ADVANCE PRAISE FOR **HR** |

"In *HR Rising!!*, Steve has again given all HR professionals a much-needed wake-up call by showing us how to be an effective leader by putting people at the very center of everything we do. A must-read for anyone at any stage in their HR career."

!! Muhammad Usman Abid, *CIPD, HR Director, Sahiwal, Pakistan*

"*HR Rising!!* inspires all HR professionals to lead from the seat they're in right now. Steve shows us it isn't just about what to do; it's about who to become."

!! Kyra Matkovich, *SHRM-CP, HR Business Partner, Madison, Wisconsin*

"Steve challenges the HR profession to Rise Up!! as legitimate leaders, gently nudging us along the way to examine what we're really doing to make things better for our organization, our people, and ourselves. Where *HR on Purpose!!* reminded us why we got into HR, *HR Rising!!* shows us how to excel."

!! Jon Thurmond, *SHRM-SCP, HR Manager, Host of #HRSocialHour podcast, Richmond, Virginia*

"Steve may be telling entertaining and enlightening stories about the evolution of and revolution in HR, but what matters more is his compelling challenge for HR professionals to rise to the occasion."

!! Heather Kinzie, *Chief Operating Officer, Anchorage, Alaska*

"A gifted storyteller, Steve Browne takes the reader through a journey of self-discovery and empowerment and motivates us to embrace the leadership potential within each of us."

!! Melanie Peacock, *PhD, MBA, CPHR, SHRM-SCP, Consultancy Owner, Calgary, Alberta, Canada*

"With characteristic positivity, energy and good humor, Steve Browne emboldens HR to be leaders in all we do. From front to back, this is a highly recommended book for everyone in the profession today."

!! Michael Carty, *MJCarty.com, Sussex, England*

HR Rising!! is the manifesto our profession needs today. Through endearing personal stories, *HR Rising!!* inspires us to put down the handbooks and begin acting like the leaders our organizations need."

!! Mike Spinale, *SHRM-SCP, Director of People Operations, Boston, Massachusetts*

"Now more than ever HR is a global community and HR Rising!! shows us what a powerful force the profession and its practitioners can be for bringing about meaningful change in the workplace."

!! Renée Robson, *Performance and Capability Manager, Melbourne, Australia*

"Steve is a wonderful, engaging storyteller and in *HR Rising!!* his stories not only educate and inspire, they'll make you laugh and encourage you to be a leader in your organization."

!! Wendy Dailey, *SHRM-CP, Talent Strategist, Host of #HRSocialHour & #HRWonderWomen podcasts, Brookings, South Dakota*

"From master storyteller Steve Browne, *HR Rising!!* invites all HR practitioners to rise up and lead the way to creating better workplaces."

!! Mofota Sefali, *Talent Brand Strategist, Johannesburg, South Africa*

HR RISING!

FROM OWNERSHIP TO LEADERSHIP

STEVE BROWNE

HR RISING!

FROM OWNERSHIP TO LEADERSHIP

STEVE BROWNE, SHRM-SCP

Society for Human Resource Management
Alexandria, Virginia
www.shrm.org

Strategic Human Resource Management India
Mumbai, India
www.shrmindia.org

Society for Human Resource Management, Middle East and Africa Office
Dubai, UAE
www.shrm.org/pages/mena.aspx

SHRM®
BETTER WORKPLACES
BETTER WORLD™

This publication is designed to provide accurate and authoritative information regarding the subject matter covered. It is sold with the understanding that neither the publisher nor the author is engaged in rendering legal or other professional service. If legal advice or other expert assistance is required, the services of a competent, licensed professional should be sought. The federal and state laws discussed in this book are subject to frequent revision and interpretation by amendments or judicial revisions that may significantly affect employer or employee rights and obligations. Readers are encouraged to seek legal counsel regarding specific policies and practices in their organizations.

This book is published by the Society for Human Resource Management (SHRM). The interpretations, conclusions, and recommendations in this book are those of the author and do not necessarily represent those of the publisher.

This publication may not be reproduced, stored in a retrieval system, or transmitted in whole or in part, in any form or by any means, electronic, mechanical, photocopying, recording, or otherwise, without the prior written permission of the publisher, or authorization through payment of the appropriate per-copy fee to the Copyright Clearance Center, Inc., 222 Rosewood Drive, Danvers, MA 01923, 978-750-8600, fax 978-646-8600, or on the Web at www.copyright.com. Requests to the publisher for permission should be addressed to SHRM Book Permissions, 1800 Duke Street, Alexandria, VA 22314, or online at http://www.shrm.org/about-shrm/pages/copyright--permissions.aspx.

SHRM books and products are available on most online bookstores and through the SHRMStore at www.shrmstore.org.

The Society for Human Resource Management is the world's largest HR professional society, representing 290,000 members in more than 165 countries. For nearly seven decades, the Society has been the leading provider of resources serving the needs of HR professionals and advancing the practice of human resource management. SHRM has more than 575 affiliated chapter within the United States and subsidiary offices in China, India, and United Arab Emirates. Please visit us at www.shrm.org.

Library of Congress Cataloging-in-Publication Data
Names: Browne, Steve, author.
Title: HR rising!! : from ownership to leadership / Steve Browne, SHRM-SCP.
Description: First Edition. | Alexandria : Society for Human Resource
   Management, 2020. | Includes index.
Identifiers: LCCN 2020010546 (print) | LCCN 2020010547 (ebook) | ISBN
   9781586446444 (paperback) | ISBN 9781586446451 (pdf) | ISBN
   9781586446468 (epub) | ISBN 9781586446475 (mobi)
Subjects: LCSH: Personnel management. | Leadership.
Classification: LCC HF5549 .B8655 2020 (print) | LCC HF5549 (ebook) | DDC 658.3--dc23

Printed in the United States of America
FIRST EDITION

PB Publishing   10 9 8 7 6 5 4 3 2 1   61.15201

DEDICATION

I'd like to dedicate this book to my Mom and Dad who set the standard of how to be positive, encouraging humans to everyone in their lives. They are the model of effortless support and love.

CONTENTS

FOREWORD

MANY, MANY YEARS AGO, when I began my career in HR, I'd never met anyone that had worked in HR (or "personnel," as it was called then). Why'd I pick that job? I wanted to work in a position where I could have the most influence and impact (as any 20-year-old would, right?), and it seemed logical to me that the one job in a company with the sole purpose of dealing with all the people would provide that opportunity. I think we can all agree that I was (admittedly) not well informed, and perhaps slightly naïve. But now, over thirty years later, I can say that my decision was absolutely the right one, and I believe more strongly today than ever before that HR is the best place to make a positive difference in any organization!

Unfortunately, I've met many people that have felt exactly the opposite. Even more unfortunately, many of those naysayers have been—you may have guessed it—HR professionals. Thankfully, after several years of working in HR, trying to remain positive in a sea of negatively, enter Steve Browne. Before I even met him in person, he was inviting me to attend the local HR association meetings and a monthly HR roundtable. He sent me a weekly email highlighting an online forum for HR leaders to ask and answer questions, and each email contained an original "HR song" that Steve had written himself. Every week.

Even as a card-carrying introvert, it was hard to avoid Steve's overwhelming positivity about the HR profession and his relentless passion about the impact that HR leaders could have in the workplace. I was reinspired by Steve to connect with why I got into HR in the first place!

For over twenty years now, I've been blessed to call Steve Browne not only a friend but a mentor. He's been a constant source of encouragement, a wise counselor during difficult times, a connector, and a great example of a positive and powerful business leader, as well as a devoted family man. He has mentored not just me but hundreds, if not thousands, of HR professionals around the world through his work as an HR executive, a blogger, a board member of the largest HR association in the world, and an author of now two best-selling books (yep, I'm confident this one will be a best seller too) in which he shares his vision of HR's positive impact and influence. And he still writes an original "HR song" in his weekly HR Net communications, which now goes out to thousands of leaders all over the world.

There are many books out there that can help you grow professionally and personally, but I'm grateful that you've chosen this one. For some of you, it will reignite your desire to be a positive influence at work and in life. For others, it will remind you of why you chose to work in HR in the first place. And for all of us, it provides encouragement to embrace the awesome opportunities that working with people can provide.

I can't wait to see what you will accomplish through the lessons learned in this book, as well as with Steve's support and encouragement as you rise!!

—Jennifer McClure
CEO of Unbridled Talent LLC
and DisruptHR LLC

A NOTE OF GRATITUDE

BEFORE YOU JUMP INTO THIS BOOK, I wanted to say, "Thank You." It may seem a bit out of place for an author to thank people prior to them reading any content. It's like a stand-up comic thanking the crowd before offering one joke. Being a contrarian, I'm good with starting in an unconventional manner.

This is my second book, which is mind-blowing to me because I never thought I'd be fortunate to write one book in my lifetime. I have been gobsmacked (a UK term for utterly astonished) by the response I have received since my first book, *HR on Purpose!!*, was published. I have received notes from HR practitioners around the globe on almost a daily basis telling me how they heard their voice finally being shared.

My hope in the first book was for my peers throughout HR to be proud of who they were and the work they do. That message has been shared with me over and over. The feedback has ranged from people stating they were going to leave this wonderful profession all the way to a group of HR pros in Pakistan putting on a 3-day *HR on Purpose!!* conference. The book is now a part of a college library, a "mandatory" read for graduate HR students in a few universities, and a read for many book clubs in SHRM chapters and businesses. A few conferences even bought copies for every attendee who came to hear me speak. I never envisioned any of this occurring.

Each time I hear from a peer, I am touched and humbled that someone was kind enough to choose to read the book. To hear that the book is seen as a reference tool for HR pros in their daily roles is simply incredible.

I have desired to see our profession come together because I think it's the best career anyone could ever experience. You get to work with people on purpose!! There is nothing better. I'm fortunate to see my first book may have provided a spark and some encouragement for HR to be more cohesive and intentionally connected globally.

For everyone who has read *HR on Purpose!!*, THANK YOU!!!! (I'm sure the editors will cringe with the multiple exclamation points, but we need to be an exuberant and passionate bunch.)

I am grateful and proud to be your peer who works alongside you. May you continue to practice HR on purpose throughout your entire career. Trust me. If you do this, you will leave a lasting impact and legacy on countless people. There is nothing more meaningful than leaving the world a better place than when you first encountered it.

INTRODUCTION

I GREW UP IN MY FORMATIVE YEARS in the village of Ada, Ohio. My mom, brother and I moved there because my mom, who had been a widow, found Don. He was a wonderful match for her, and he asked her to be his wife. Don became our "dad" quickly because he became such a great influence and presence in our lives. He was never our step-dad. He was, and is, the real deal!!

During the summer between my freshman and sophomore year of college, I didn't have a job. My dad was never one to let us idly sit around the house because he had such a strong work ethic. He expected the same high level of work from myself and my brother. My brother got a "pass" that summer because he was still in high school and had other activities during the summer.

One morning my dad came into my room and told me to put on some clothes that could get dirty. He had a project for me. At the time, my parents owned a second home in town, which they rented out to long-term tenants or graduate students from the local university. We ate a large breakfast and got in his El Camino to drive across town to the house and the impending project.

The "green house," as we called it, was an old house. It was rock solid and so well-built that it was never going to fall into disrepair. However, my dad wanted to update the units to make them more modern. The project for this summer was going to be the renovation of the upstairs unit. The house had two more units on the first floor that had already been updated.

As we pulled up and parked, Dad told me to grab the tools out of the bed of the El Camino and follow him upstairs. I did as I was told and trudged up the stairs with my arms full of a hammer, five-gallon buckets, and other small hand tools. The second floor had bare floors and clean walls. I had no idea what needed to be done. It all looked fine to me.

One quick aside . . .

I'm not really a hands-on person. My dad had grown up on a farm outside of town, and he was always doing projects that involved hard work and a ton of manual labor. If he didn't know how to do something, he taught himself or had his dad teach him. I grew up "in town" and was active in every possible area of school I could be. That included sports, choir, and clubs. I never had to do manual work because my dad took care of those tasks. I'd lend a hand, but I never had to do a project on my own.

Back to the action . . .

My dad said, "Today we're going to tear down the plaster and lathe on these walls. And by 'we,' I mean you."

Although the walls seemed perfectly fine to me, he explained that the plaster was decades old and that people now expected drywall and insulation in their walls. He wanted the plaster removed so we could add that. I shrugged and asked him what to do.

He took a hammer and hit the wall with some serious force. The plaster cracked and fell into chunks on the floor. Behind the plaster were small, horizontal slats the plaster had been adhered to. Dad took a pry bar and popped a few of the slats out of the hole he had just made.

"That's it," he said. "Keep taking down the plaster and the lathe slats. Put the stuff you take off the walls into the five-gallon buckets. Take the buckets downstairs and empty them into the dumpster."

"That's all?" I responded.

"Yep. I'll come check on you at lunch time. We'll go and grab something to eat, and then you can come back to tearing down the walls. Oh, and I brought you a radio. I know you like listening to music all the time. Just get the work done."

He descended the stairs and left to go to work. I put on a mask to protect me from the plaster dust, turned on my fave rock station, and started to hack away at the wall. It was tiring work!! Plaster and lathe last for decades because they are a thick, sturdy combination. The hole my dad started did get bigger, but it was slow going. After working for hours, I had made a hole about five feet tall and four feet wide. I'd cleaned up the waste and had a fairly clean working space even though I was covered in white dust from head to toe. I looked like I had been dipped in flour.

I heard my dad tromping up the steps in his work boots and was eager to show him my progress. When he got up to the second floor, he just stared, and his mouth dropped open.

"Is that all?" he asked, obviously irritated.

"Yeah," I threw back indignantly.

"Did you even work the entire time I've been gone?" His frustration was boiling now.

I was just as frustrated and snapped back at him. "I haven't stopped since you left. Why are you so upset?"

He just couldn't believe that I had done so little in the hours that had passed. He insinuated that I was a slacker, then he disappeared down a short hallway behind the wall I had been working on destroying. He reappeared with a sledgehammer in his hands.

He started swinging it directly into the plaster and demolished a giant section of the wall with a mere four or five swings. He turned on me, breathing heavily, and retorted, "That's how you take down a wall!!"

I was furious. "Well, how the hell did you expect me to tear down the wall when I didn't know we had a sledgehammer up here?"

"You knew it was here," he snapped back.

"I did not!! All I had was this regular hammer and this pry bar. I did just what you showed me." Tears welled up in my eyes and made streaks in the plaster dust that I was covered in. "You didn't tell me. You didn't." I stormed away and stood in the yard. We both calmed down, and he asked me if I knew what to do now. I was still pissed and gave a short grunt and went back upstairs. He had brought me a sandwich and a soda from the convenient store a block down the road, but I didn't eat it.

I picked up the sledgehammer and hit the wall over and over and over. I cleared out half of the room and took down two full walls in a matter of minutes. I was still crying as I swung that sledgehammer. I was "working" but purely out of anger. After this mad flurry of smashing the plaster and lathe, I dropped the hammer, exhausted. My dad had already returned to work, telling me he'd be back at dinner time.

I calmed down, ate the sandwich, and continued doing the project correctly now that I had received full instructions. When Dad returned at dinner time, I had finished taking down a room and a half. He was pleased and we drove back home for dinner.

Now, don't think poorly of my dad. He's an amazing person and I'm grateful for him. Without him, I would never had understood the power of a strong work ethic. I am a better man because of his example of how to do things well from start to finish.

However, the plaster/lathe debacle is indicative of how we interact as HR professionals in today's organizations. We act just like I did in this situation. We want to be involved in the necessary work of the company, and we are excited about having a role that will make a difference. We get whatever instruction is given, and then we do our best.

My dad's reaction is typical of how senior leadership and other departments respond to us when they think we don't "get it." Why didn't we look for other ways to do the work in front of us? Why didn't we question the methods explained to us to see whether we had all of the information we needed? Why didn't we take the time to see whether the expectations of the person(s) in charge were defined and clear?

You can come up with more and more questions. The reason we're always in this secondary position is because we refuse to lead. We have fallen into the trap, and myth, that HR is only meant to be a support function. We feel that if we just work hard and stay in our place, then others will recognize our efforts and reward us for a job well done.

This has never worked. Ever.

HR must lead. I'm not talking about some mystical leadership program or method that assures our ascension to become a VP or a CHRO. That isn't leadership. It may be career advancement, but we should never assume level or title automatically infers "leadership."

I know there are countless books, blogs, conference sessions, and models that include three, five, seven, or ten steps that ensure you *will* become a leader. This book won't have that. Not in the least.

I do believe we are called to lead as human resource professionals. We need to lead because our roles are intertwined with the most prevalent and valued resource of a company: its people.

I want to walk down the short hall and get out the sledgehammer that I should have shown you when you started down this path. Throughout this book I'm going to lay out attributes I feel will help you lead from where you are, regardless of the level of the role you currently hold. These various characteristics can be applied in every type of industry, and wherever you work, you'll see them present.

The key to starting this journey and leading as a human resources professional is to see which of these attributes fit your work experience. Put together what works for you and start to act. You need to stop looking for the perfect model or silver bullet to mimic. Leadership starts with who you are as a person, not from some magic formula.

I'm geeked to let you know that I believe in what you do as a fellow professional who happens to be in HR. My hope is that the pages that follow will equip you to tear down the walls of the past and launch yourself into a position that shows how talented you've always been.

Now, let's pick up that sledgehammer and start swinging!!

CHAPTER 1

PASSIVE NO LONGER

ONE OF THE MANY THINGS I loved about growing up in a small town was that you could be involved in as many clubs, sports, and activities as you wanted to in high school. I have always enjoyed being well-rounded and comfortable in a variety of settings. During my high school years, I was active in everything from serving in student government to performing in the school musicals and show choir. I took the most advanced classes offered and enjoyed chemistry, calculus, physics, and advanced English studying classics.

I was also fortunate to be on a very good basketball team. Our school won seven conference titles in a row, and I was on three of those teams. We did well in the first rounds of the end-of-year tournaments for the state title, but unfortunately, we fell short by one point just one game from earning a place in the final four.

My senior year was especially memorable. I had been playing with most of my teammates since seventh grade, and this was our chance to be the leaders. We had worked hard for years and wanted to win another title. Now, I need to digress for just a bit . . .

I played in a time when coaches were very vocal and not always positive. My coach was more typical of the "yell and demean" approach, which was prevalent in both high school and college sports. If I had to guess, it's probably how he was coached. He had been very successful for years, so I assume he felt this approach was effective because the kids always performed well and won more often than not. He was rough on all the players, including his sons when they came through the program.

Coach liked athletes to be athletes and little else. He felt you should be fully dedicated to his program only. I didn't fit that mold. Some of my fantastic teammates were more focused on sports than me, so I was the target of his ire and strings of obscenities during practices and games. He called me soft, weak, and things I'd rather not repeat. I never talked back to him or complained. He swore he would break me and "make me a man" through his constant badgering. I would just take a deep breath and keep playing.

During one of our final conference games, I was having the best game I ever had played. I had double-digit points and rebounds and had even blocked a few shots of our opponent. I was geeked that things were going so well. As halftime came, our team went to the locker room to rest and get ready for the second half. My teammates and I exchanged high fives, and they encouraged me to have an even better second half. All of them took a seat on a bench, and I was the last player in. I turned around to sit down when my coach's rolled-up towel crashed across my face. He had wound up and intentionally struck me. I lost my balance a bit but gathered myself and looked him straight in the eye and chin to chin. My teammates were itching to jump up and defend me, but they waited for my reaction.

I shook my head, laughed, and took my place on the bench with my team. He wasn't expecting this response. It infuriated him even more!! He leaned down and screamed every blue word possible with his sweat and spit landing on my face. I never said a word and never looked away. My fellow post player, Richard, spoke up, "Coach, why are you screaming at Steve? If it wasn't for him, we'd be getting crushed out there. He's having a great game. We're the ones who should be playing better."

My coach turned to Richard, his eyes bulging and the veins in his neck protruding. He didn't yell at Richard. He calmed down and walked away. Richard leaned over and said, "I wanted to jump up and hit him back. He shouldn't have done that." I replied, "I know, Rich. But he wanted me to react and be like him. I'm never going to do that."

We went on to win the game and the conference title. At the end of the season, Coach handed me a co-MVP plaque, and I was named to the all-star team for the conference and district along with many of my teammates.

I never told my parents that the coach had hit me until a few years later while I was in college. I actually saw Coach at church. I know ironic but true. He had mellowed out and asked me how school was. I was respectful and told him it was going well and it was great to see him.

This incident made such a lasting impression on me. I didn't realize that leadership would resemble my basketball coach more than other models on several occasions in my career. They weren't nearly as colorful in their language, but it's happened. I've experienced this personally and I've often seen leaders take a rough stance with their direct reports. For the first part of my career, I didn't feel it was HR's role to get involved. In fact, I was told that HR should stay "in its place" and I would be summoned to be involved only when needed. I didn't question this approach or sentiment about HR . . . at first.

> **For far too long, HR has been willingly ostracized in organizations.**

For far too long, HR has been willingly ostracized in organizations. We have allowed ourselves to be relegated to the sidelines and fringes of the daily business world swirling all around us. We've been content with this, and we haven't wanted to push back. Our concern for on-going employment has outweighed the urge to change this status.

This complacency needs to change. We are essential to the team that makes our organization thrive and succeed. It's time we stepped out and rose to a position of leadership and integration. We can't let the company overlook us anymore.

I held one job where I was an HR department of one for a family owned manufacturing company. We did heavy machining in one location and welding in another location on extremely large pieces. I was responsible for the safety initiatives and overall program for our two plants. At the welding facility, there were overhead cranes which ran on tracks secured over 25 feet in the air. Each crane had a weight capacity listed on the track. Even though they were able to hoist and secure pieces weighing several tons, the welders were often asked to maneuver pieces that exceeded the capacity. I saw this potentially lethal hazard and stopped production. The supervisor was hacked because he knew he'd get yelled at for stopping work. I told him I didn't care because the safety of our employees was far more important than continuing work in the manner they were following.

I went to the plant manager and told him that stopping production was my decision. He instantly became worried. He knew the senior leaders of the company would come down on him if he missed a deadline. I told him I understood, but we had to make sure people were safe first. I wanted the work to be completed, but not at the expense of someone potentially getting hurt or killed. I explained this wasn't an exaggeration. If the crane failed because of too much weight, the mechanism could crash to the ground or the chains holding the piece could fail and shoot across the room.

I reassured the plant manager and told him I would go to the senior leadership and give them my reasoning for stopping the job. I drove back to my office at the machining plant and went to the President of the company. He was a family member and one of five sons who "ran" the company. I say that loosely because this family was far more concerned with how the family members lined their pockets than the actual work being done by the good employees of the company.

He was furious and told me I had no authority to stop the job. I kept my cool and disagreed. I was direct with him. I informed him that this safety violation was reckless. I couldn't allow him to put people in harm's way. He threatened to fire me on the spot, and I retorted that I would contact OSHA and file a complaint myself.

"You're the head of HR of my company! You do what I say, and you represent us. You can't report us," he screamed with his face now a beet red and veins protruding from his neck.

"I'm responsible for everyone. All of our employees. All of them. I will contact them if you don't address this." I was shaking on the inside, but I knew I had to do what was right.

"Get out of my office!" he bellowed.

I turned and walked out and went back to my desk. He did back down and went out to the welding facility. I'm sure he described me in very colorful language with the plant manager, but he made sure that changes occurred to ensure the safety of our workers.

The project was completed, and no one was hurt. I was grateful he did what was needed.

It took courage to stand up to the head of the company. He could have fired me and done nothing. I also could have done nothing and hoped no one would have been injured. I chose to rise up and lead instead.

HR professionals are meant to be well-rounded resources. We can't be confined to one narrow aspect of our job. We can perform at all levels of our company regardless of our roles and titles. We need to see ourselves in broader terms because we should be leaders who bring our teams together across departments. The canvas and reach of HR is limitless. I mean it. Break out of the stagnant position in which you've been entrenched. It's isn't helping you or the people who need you.

In this book, I'm going to share a variety of approaches that will allow you to reshape how you practice HR. I hope you'll see that you are critical to the success of others throughout your company. To realize who you can be you need to take a stand and rally others on purpose.

Your employees are waiting for this. We can no longer be passive personally, as a profession or as an industry. *Rise up!!*

CHAPTER 2

TAKE A CHANCE ON ME

DO YOU REMEMBER disco music? I do because I lived through it, and I'm here to admit that I loved it as well!! Every disco song had a fierce beat keeping the genre upbeat and positive. One of the superstars of the disco movement was the Swedish group ABBA. Their songs were pop music masterpieces filled with catchy lyrics that were easy to memorize. If you're an ABBA fan, you can sing every song from the moment it starts playing.

One of their biggest and most well-known hits is "Take a Chance on Me." The lyrics express one person's availability and hope of having a relationship with someone else.

You never know if the couple connects and gets together, but you are hopeful that they do. Regardless of the outcome, the person singing the song is voicing their interest and stating that they're available. Does this approach make you uncomfortable and a bit tingly? For many, being so "forward" is not in their nature, especially when looking at this from a perspective within an organization.

As HR practitioners, we are conditioned to fall into place. We have defined roles and the expectation is for us to stay within the lines written in some form of a job description. Since we feel this is the only area from which we can perform, we in turn force this narrow approach on others as well. Everyone in their place. No exceptions. We tend to get highly agitated when people decide to work outside of these defined parameters.

> **As HR practitioners, we are conditioned to fall into place.**

Another factor that influences our internal professional limitations is that we're nice and polite. Isn't it awful that these attributes are viewed as negatives? They are viewed in a negative light because we have mistakenly labeled "empathy" as a soft skill. Empathy is a business skill, and it always has been. It should be present across the entire enterprise and not just seen as the warm and fuzzy side of HR. It's a shame that the emotional side of our profession restricts our growth in the eyes of others.

What's even more disconcerting is the fact we don't fight the button-holing of our profession. We may hem and haw in the isolation of our office, but we tend to shrug our shoulders and step in line. I have spoken with countless HR professionals in person, online, and at HR conferences who are tired of feeling like they're relegated to a tight set of position boundaries. They want to step out of this corral, but they don't know how to do it.

Let me suggest this: listen to ABBA. Show the organization why it should *take a chance* on you as a leader who is willing and able to work outside the parameters of HR. This involves some risk taking and a willingness to be vulnerable and even stumble along the way. Unfortunately, the call for the company to take a chance on you requires initiative on your part. If you continue to sit and wait for some magic day when senior leadership wakes up and sees you're an incredibly talented professional, you may be waiting your entire career.

Stepping forward and asking for a larger role or a bigger reach doesn't make you less empathetic. In fact, being courageous will only benefit you. Know that you will face some skepticism and questions from others wondering why HR is working outside their normal world. It's natural. You need to assure your coworkers you're bringing the "people perspective" to projects. The vast majority of all activity that occurs in companies involves people at some level. I'm sure there are a few non-people functions, but they are the exception.

Courage is risky. You need to put yourself out there because if you don't, you will never be seen. It's ironic that almost every other profession has no

> **Courage is risky. You need to put yourself out there because if you don't, you will never be seen.**

problem stepping forward. They seek to broaden their horizons and take on larger roles. HR has to stop acting like a shrinking violet. It has hindered how we're seen and how we're treated. We need to quit the practice of departments only working with HR when they "have to." Stepping out into the space where others are already working is the solution you need to embrace.

What does this look like in your current situation? I'm not sure, to be honest. Each HR role is unique. This is true because of the people who occupy these roles and also because of how your company currently views the scope of what Human Resources should be doing. If you take the first step and no longer allow HR to be a last-minute, forced choice when involved, you'll make incredible progress. You should be confident in how HR is viewed. This shouldn't be defined by others. You can give life to your entire function, whether you're a giant department or a department of one, by starting your journey of professional courage here.

The next step forward is up to you. I can't presuppose your culture, situation, or circumstance. This doesn't mean the next step is vague, but it is up to you to assess your environment and decide where you should go next. It won't be prescriptive. Taking this action may make you uncomfortable, but asking others to take a chance on you is always mixed with uncertainty. A bit of anxiety will be present any time you venture forward. Remember this anytime you encourage others to step up. We are good at telling others to have courage, but we are hesitant when it comes to being courageous ourselves.

It's time for you to be the first in line. Let others know you're still free and it's time for them to take a chance on you!!

CHAPTER 3

BE THE YEAST

HAVE YOU EVER ENJOYED the smell of fresh baked bread? The aroma is so inviting that your mouth will begin to water, and you'll seek it out. You'll search and search to see where the bread is being baked just to get another whiff of this comforting smell.

My early years were spent on my grandparent's farm in the tiny village of Luckey, Ohio. (Seriously, you can Google the location.) My grandfather raised dairy cows and also had several acres of corn, wheat, and hay. He woke at dawn every day and went out to either the barn or the fields for the day. When our mom was at work, my brother and I were regular spectators to all the farm had to offer. You see, our father had passed away at the tender age of 26. He was a Vietnam veteran and a wonderful dad and husband. He contracted non-Hodgkins lymphoma, which may have been due to exposure to Agent Orange during serving in a battle, but that's a story for another time. My brother was two years old and I was four years old when he passed.

Fortunately, my extended family is extremely close and supportive. They understand that "life" happens all around us, so my grandparents were willing caretakers while my mom earned a living. She would get us ready for the day and take us from our house trailer located a mile away from the farm and get us settled in. We loved being on the farm!! The constant activity, sounds, and smells provided an endless land of adventure for two young boys. We were too young to be very effective in helping around the farm, but Grandpa and Grandma made sure we were lending a hand instead of sitting in front of a television.

While Grandpa was out of the house, Grandma ruled. She ran the entire house with ease and joy. Everything back then was done by hand and from scratch. She didn't have the technology we enjoy today, but she loved baking and cooking. Her kitchen was something to behold. There always seemed to be something bubbling and brewing on the stovetop while something else was baking in the oven.

One thing my brother and I loved to help our Grandma make was bread. Grandma would get out her massive "bread making" blue bowl and then get the sifter out. Many people these days don't know what a sifter is. She'd measure out the flour she needed and put it in the sifter. It had a crank on the side, and you'd turn it clockwise to sift the flour and make it just right for baking. This was one of our tasks, and we loved cranking the sifter because we usually ended up with flour all over our faces and shirts. Once the flour sifting was completed, Grandma would add a dash of salt and some water. Then the fun began!! She'd stir the slurry into a sticky, gooey dough, which would fiercely cling to the spoon. She'd nod and give us permission to pull out the dough and knead it with our hands. It was heaven because we were there with one of our favorite humans on the planet doing something that added value to the household. Our hard work would soon be baked and brought to the table to share with Grandpa once he came in from a hard day out on the farm.

After several minutes of furious kneading, my brother and I were eager to put the dough into bread pans so they could become golden loaves of goodness. Grandma would tell us to slow down because the most critical ingredient was missing. We were perplexed. We had sifted the flour, added the water, and kneaded the dough. What could be needed? The answer was the yeast.

Grandma would go to her pantry and pull out a small red, yellow, and white envelope with the brand name, Fleishman's, emblazoned across the front of the package. It seemed insignificant and silly. How could something so small be necessary? She didn't explain it fully at the time instead saying, "You need to be patient. Yeast takes time to do its magic." She gently tore open the envelope and emptied a minute number of brown granules into the mass of dough that was evidently "in progress." She'd take a cotton towel, place it over the bowl, and tell us to go play outside.

That was it? We were confused. It didn't look like or smell like bread. We'd head outside for new adventures and come back in a few hours later. When we did, we were amazed at what we witnessed. The ball of dough we had pounded into submission was now three times its size. Grandma would ask us to wash up and come help her. We'd put Crisco all over our hands and grease the loaf pans waiting to be filled. She always did the last step of taking the now risen dough and splitting it into the exact size needed to fill the pans. Into the oven they'd go, and after a short time, the smell we had anticipated would begin to waft through the kitchen.

Once Grandpa had returned and mealtime finally arrived, Grandma would get out her electric knife and cut just enough slices of bread for each of us. It was savored every, single time.

Making bread with my Grandma is how leadership should be in organizations. She never followed a set recipe because she knew the ingredients and the process by memory. It was taught to her by her mother and she, in turn, taught the method to us. Not one step was missed or rushed. Not one. We tried to cut corners so we could get to the final result, but she knew better.

Organizational leadership often lacks patience because of the assumption that there is never enough time. Work is either behind, out of order, or incomplete. No one challenges this assumption. It's just continuously followed. This rush to finish leads to frustration, stagnation, and complaining by all those involved. The leader who is responsible for the work at hand feels immeasurable pressure, real or not, which makes the people they're leading also feel pressed to rush. If the leader is running, they expect everyone else to run as well.

HR needs to be like my Grandma. We need to be the ones who know the processes by heart so that we can calm folks down and let them know there is always enough time. Rarely is there such a critical deadline unless someone has neglected their work entirely. That's a different issue and, honestly, a performance discussion. If HR would assume the mantle of leading through their work and interactions with others, then they could help set the pace needed for the tasks at hand. This would be true in their department as well as assisting other departmental leaders as a model for them.

My grandmother knew what needed to happen for the bread to be made well. She slowed us down even though we were eager to push ahead. She appreciated our passion and willingness to work, but she was able to lead us at a pace that was both forward-focused and efficient. Organizations strive for this but rarely attain on a consistent basis.

She also kept the key ingredient to herself. My brother and I were more than capable of getting the yeast packet from the pantry and emptying it into the dough. However, she never gave that task up. She was astute to build in this barometer check for two reasons. She wanted to make sure we were paying attention to the process and remind us we shouldn't be so rushed as to forget such an important step. So often in today's workplace, we overlook the small ingredients because we don't think they're meaningful enough to make a difference. We think if we skip over the yeast, it won't matter. Well, it does because without it, you'll never get the dough to the proper place in order for it to reach its final destination.

HR practitioners are reluctant to lead because we've believed the misconception that "leadership" takes some monumental effort. It has to be vibrant, charismatic, and noticed by one and all. This has never been true. We need to be the yeast. HR can provide the key ingredient to leadership themselves by showing others that they are needed before things move forward. Now, this takes courage because it calls you to be intentional by stepping into interactions which may not directly involve HR-related work.

If you do this, you'll see how critical and essential HR is. By helping others slow down, breathe, reflect, and check to make sure all the ingredients are in place, you are leading far more than you think. Practicing this behavior may seem daunting, and your organization may question why HR is acting in this manner. The reason HR should step in is because companies keep sprinting so much that they blow past tangible results that could be built upon. Sure, things are "getting done," but how effectively?

It only takes a small amount of attention and connectivity to help collaboration. You can be the yeast. You can be the one, small influence that gets work unstuck and moving forward. It's time for HR to understand that it can be the key ingredient in allowing work to continue to flow. This simple action will yield consistent results, and in the end, exhibit leadership.

CHAPTER 4

DO YOU HAVE A SECOND?

ONE OF THE BENCHMARKS of workplace culture is the "Open
Door Policy." It is well intentioned, but rarely followed. I find it
unusual that companies have decided to make accessibility to
other coworkers a "policy." Does that mean your open-door policy
should have the same weight as other policies which could lead
to discipline or termination? Of course not.

Companies make sure this policy is present in their employee
handbook because they're trying to communicate that they desire
an open environment of communication. This is meant to be true
for any employee at any level at any time. It's a utopian aspiration
that just isn't practiced. It can't be for several legitimate reasons.

The first reason is that people are hesitant to be open to others
because they feel the pressure to get things done. Productivity
is valued far more than any other attribute in an organization.
When people can crank out work product, they are viewed as
being a strong contributor who understands what it means
to perform. This attribute carries such power that it often
leads to higher compensation and even more significant roles.
Production, by itself, is hard to argue against. If the quality of a
mass-producer is spot-on, they are quickly moved up past others
who produce less.

The more focus a company has on production for production's
sake, the less time we have for interacting with others. Therefore,
the door needs to be closed in order for production to exist at
its peak.

Secondly, people don't want to talk to people. This sounds harsh,
but it's true. When two people encounter each other, there's a
likelihood that the conversation will be inane or courteous. We
feel the pressure to "get back to work." It's interesting to note that
for people to truly perform, they require interaction and contributions from at least one other person on a regular basis. Taking
time out of our day to have these "frivolous" conversations not
directly related to the work is seen as wasting time. Can you see
the door shutting again?

The third reason is that people are constantly interrupted. If they aren't personally interrupted, chances are they're interrupting someone else. This is rarely malicious. We are so self-focused that we don't see that when we talk with someone else, we're distracting them from the work they were in the process of doing. We honestly think we are just quickly touching base to garner the snippet of input, feedback, or information we need before we scurry back to work. The moment we return and continue our tasks, someone else interrupts us.

This reality is so frustrating, and people audibly complain about never having enough time to themselves to be productive. Now the door is barely cracked open. There is a sliver of light coming through, so we feel content that our door is open enough. Does this sound like your experience and work environment?

Instead of addressing the reality of constant interruptions, people work harder and harder to try and push any distraction away. We dream of a space where we can solely focus on what's important to us and pray no one enters our perfect habitat. This idyllic space may sound perfect, but it isn't realistic.

It's time we come to terms with this fact. Work happens in the middle of interruptions. It always has. We relish distractions. We either are eager to have them occur or we seek them out. For most jobs, work done in complete, or semi-complete, isolation isn't possible. Work without interruptions also limits the effectiveness of production. We need to have interactions with others. We try out ideas with our coworkers. We look for affirmation and acknowledgement. Why? It's simple. Because we're humans, and we are interdependent in order to drive results.

Since we're being pulled in many ways which are rarely related to each other in the course of a "normal" day, how can we lead effectively?

The traditional reaction is to suggest people put dedicated time in their schedule to ensure they are free of interruptions. We encourage people to block out their calendars for "me time." This approach may work to some extent, but it's challenging to do this to any sort of scale because people aren't able to coordinate their scheduled interruption-free time to coincide with others. It does feel good to have that block of peace during a day, so you may want to do this as one option in handling interruptions, but don't make it the only approach. Sprinkle it in every so often.

At the beginning of my career, I learned how to work within interruptions from a very harsh lesson. I was working in a staunch, rigid corporate workplace in my first HR role. Every movement seemed to be scripted and done in an orderly, linear manner. Communication used a myriad of internal acronyms on paper memos. Most communication was done at arm's length, which made it impersonal and limited. You rarely had any context on the interoffice memos that moved from inbox to inbox. You were supposed to figure out the meaning behind the sparse wording on your own.

I didn't understand this method, and I felt confused and lost. It got so bad that I didn't feel I was able to do my job as a recruiter at all. The internal acronym code had me baffled. Since I felt I was daily walking through a fog, I decided to go against the norm. I grabbed a handful of the mysterious memos and walked straight into my boss's office. I didn't pause or hesitate to ask if he had time to answer my questions. I can remember him looking up from his work with narrowed eyes and protruding wrinkles on his forehead. It didn't slow me one bit.

"Hey, Bob, I have some questions about these memos. I just don't understand them."

"Stop right there!" I was surprised by his terse response. I thought I was being eager and curious. Again, I was clueless about how rude I was being.

"Steve, leave my office and start over."

"What? What did I do wrong?"

"Just go back out and start this conversation over."

Now I was the one who had narrowed eyes and a furrowed brow. I stomped out of his office like an upset four year old. I turned around and went to reenter his office. Just as I reached the door's threshold, he said, "Wait."

I almost tripped over myself with the sudden stop. "What?" I was becoming more and more frustrated.

"Ask me if I have a second to see you."

I was floored. All I wanted was to have my simple questions answered. I was sure what I was going to ask wasn't going to take hours of his time. What was the big deal?

"I mean it. Ask me."

I sighed, shrugged and said, "Bob, do you have a second to see me?"

"Sure, come on in. What can I do for you?"

Then the light bulb clicked. He wasn't being difficult or aloof. He wanted me to see if he could be interrupted. He wanted me to respect his time instead of barging in to just get my quick answer so I could run back to my desk to continue my work. He saw that I understood, and he said something I've tried to remember, and practice, ever since.

"Remember that everyone's time is important. Not just yours."

He answered my questions and gave me the clarity I was looking for in understanding how our internal communication process worked. He also taught me how to lead during interruptions.

Interruptions are going to occur whether you want them to or not. You have the opportunity in your role as HR to help guide others on how to work within this reality. Teach others to pause, ask if someone has a second, then respect their time. You have more time available to you each day than you think. This mad dash approach has never been effective.

From now on, breathe, pause, and ask, "Do you have a second?"

Chances are the other person does. If they don't, your question gives them the chance to gracefully bow out and ask to follow up with you later. The key is to hold people accountable and follow up with them.

If you make the time to teach people how to have good interactions, then the interruptions turn into the normal flow of work they were meant to be. You're also going to be able to open your door to welcome others in all the time.

CHAPTER 5

THE TARPIT OF AMBIGUITY

WHEN I WAS A YOUNG BOY, I fondly remember playing with toy dinosaurs. I had a huge set of them ranging from pterodactyls to a T-Rex or two. I would set up scenes where they would be scattered all over the family room floor. I'd make up adventures, and they would inevitably end up attacking each other. Since I enjoyed the set so much, my mom purchased another that was made up of various prehistoric mammals. I had saber-tooth tigers, giant sloths, and of course, woolly mammoths.

I was consumed with these toys and wanted to learn more about them. I would check books out of the school library and read anything I could get my hands on. From these books I learned about the famous La Brea tar pits located in California. The tar pits were large pools of sticky ooze, which would capture animals who unknowingly wandered into them. Once these creatures got stuck in the tar, they'd fight more and more, which led to them getting even more trapped. The tar pits were unforgiving, and many animals met their untimely death there. There's a fantastic museum located in Hancock Park today where the tar pits still exist.

Even though woolly mammoths no longer roam the earth, tar pits still are in existence. In fact, they are present in every organization. Like the bubbly mire of the La Brea tar pits, people don't see the ones lying around within companies until it's too late. These traps seem to swallow people on a regular basis.

The cause for the modern-day tar pit isn't an oily black goo; it's ambiguity. As you walk through your normal workday, you're surrounded by ambiguity. People talk in vague terms that lack any sense of clarity. We all seem to sense this lack of clarity, but we rarely question it. Instead of trying to get more concrete answers, we just try to figure out situations on our own. We are reluctant to ask for clarity because others say they "get it" even though they're as confused as you are.

The power and reach of ambiguity are significant. There are people who fill senior roles who never seem to have much substance. Yes, they have a title which presumes authority, but when you interact with them it feels like they are very good at being colorful, descriptive, and vapid at the same time. Many people give the obligatory nod of agreement while you look at them perplexed about what they said. You feel you're in the minority, so you don't question them. The peer pressure is too great, and everyone justifies this inactivity because the person holds a senior role. They "must" know what they're doing because they have a senior role.

Ambiguity also occurs between peers and in projects. There are countless meetings that are slow, methodical, and usually a waste of time. People share just enough information to make sure they're participating and getting credit from the team leader, whether what they share is meaningful or not. People get frustrated in the midst of this incremental inactivity, and they either stop moving or shift in another direction.

Ambiguity is silent and yet so prevalent that countless organizations become stagnate because of it. Sure, people are busy with work, but is the "right" work being completed? Once companies become stuck, they are easy prey just like the woolly mammoth. The saber-tooth tigers of competitors are prowling around the tar pits just waiting for a chance to pounce. Ambiguity must brought out of the shadows and addressed.

HR has a chance to be the beacon of light to expose this detrimental behavior. However, before we talk about how this can be incorporated into human resources roles, we need to confront the largest tar pit of ambiguity that exists in every single company. It's us—human resources.

We generate more goo and tar to get people stuck than any other discipline. It's not even close. During some "prehistoric" time of the profession, an HR practitioner decided to give a vague response to someone who was seeking clarity on an employee issue. This was done with good intentions because there was probably a fear that if HR committed to a decision, then someone would disagree or push back. This ambiguity relieved the pressure of the situation at hand and everyone felt good about the release of tension. A small portion of the situation was resolved, and people moved on.

Sound familiar?

When HR takes this "lead with vagueness" approach, ambiguity ensues. It's great that people feel good and tension is lessened, but a lack of decisiveness is not a good outcome. This approach leads to on-going waffling. Short-term relief never leads to long-term resolution. HR should be consistent and consider all aspects of employee situations, but then it needs to be decisive!! We can't expect ambiguity to disappear, or be addressed, if we're the most ambiguous group in the company.

> We can't expect ambiguity to disappear, or be addressed, if we're the most ambiguous group in the company.

I know I have been the person who's given a vague answer to buy time. It's a great defense mechanism, but it also puts us in a diminished position within the organization. If others feel they're going to get a lukewarm, semi-accurate response when they work with HR, they'll either start avoiding us or, even worse, handling HR items on their own.

We can make a monumental impact on how companies communicate and interact by clearing up the ambiguity flowing everywhere. Remember this: being clear does not mean you must be harsh. We can't keep thinking that providing clarity will result in cold, callous outcomes. Bringing clarity to the workplace across departments and in the middle of on-going projects may be the single most needed business skill you can possess.

The key is to recognize when communication is blurry and nondescript. If you see this, then step in and take the steps needed to gain more clarity. Ask tough questions and get people to commit to their ideas. Let them know it's safe to do this and that it needs to be the new norm when we work together. It may feel awkward and bumpy at first, but it works.

One thing to keep in mind when you're removing the tar pits that exist in your HR practice and in your organization is that it's a constant and endless effort. This may seem daunting or discouraging, but it's a fact. Ambiguity is prevalent because it's never acknowledged or challenged. Once you begin the cleanup, understand that it takes a ton of focus and consistency in order for it to be removed. However, it's worth it.

From now on, don't let people get stuck in the goo. Be the person, and department, who shows a better environment for work to occur. Be clear in all you do.

CHAPTER 6

MESSY AND WONDERFUL

HAVE YOU EVER SEEN A CHILD in front of a cake at their first birthday? Everyone is anticipating that the child will dig in, and phones are out to record the momentous occasion. The parents are excited but also a bit anxious because they're not sure if their child will "perform" or not. The one year old is mesmerized by the flame of the single lit candle and startled by everyone singing loudly. The birthday song comes to a close, the mom or dad leans in to show the child how to blow out a candle, and everyone quiets down to see what will happen.

The child is intrigued by this whole situation and isn't very focused. Once the ruckus calms down, they look at the piece of cake slathered with thick frosting. They tentatively reach out and dip one finger into the frosting, and instantly put the covered digit into their mouth. Their eyes widen when they realize this item in front of them is sweet goodness. The next action is when the phone videos start rolling in earnest because the child completely forgets anyone else exists in the room with them. They dive in with both hands in an absolute frenzy. Large chunks of cake and frosting are launched into their eager mouth, and they can't eat fast enough. Most of the cake never makes it to their mouth. The child sits gleefully with frosting smeared over their entire face and high chair. They giggle and giggle because everyone watching is happy to see this young child enjoying their birthday treat to its fullest.

Interestingly enough, no one corrects the child during this celebration. The fact is that the people who gathered for the one year old's birthday would have been sorely disappointed if the child didn't cover themselves in cake and frosting. Imagine the reaction of everyone if the child properly picked up a fork and slowly ate their cake with couth and decorum. The same result of consuming the treat would have occurred, but the life, energy, and joy would have been missing. We would wonder what went wrong, and how someone so young had become so reserved and confined when they should have been ecstatic.

Fast forward when the one year old has now aged and has joined the workforce. The same person who was allowed to be exuberant is now expected to be reserved and stay in their place. There is little room for them to be expressive because of company norms that press in from every angle. Countless systems define all aspects of this person's day from the time it starts, to when they're allowed to take breaks or enjoy a meal, to when they're released to go home. There are also limitations on whom they're allowed to interact with. The reality of position, alleged power, and levels of authority limit the movement and daily interaction of this once curious child because they are now an employee.

Why have organizations become so strict and sterile? Why has "work" become something that has to be regimented and rigid? So much time is spent keeping people in line and conforming to a mix of rules that are made for the few instead of the majority. The pressure to fit in is as heavy as any performance expectation. I understand there are companies that exist which have colorful work environments and countless "benefits" from unlimited PTO to unstructured work schedules, but even in the most forward-thinking company, there is still the allure of "control."

Managers and those in senior roles feel compelled to make sure their assets are "accountable," which really means that they need people to conform to their style and approach. We want people who aren't messy. We are convinced that the more people fit in, the less variability will occur. We're innately afraid that if we give employees the permission to work on their own, chaos is sure to consume the entire company culture and lead to the demise of the organization. Insert skeptical belly laugh here.

Has this ever happened? Did the one year old who smashed cake in their face with unadulterated joy turn out to be a train wreck of a person? Did that lay the groundwork for a lifetime of endless unpredictable behavior? The answer is no.

Now, I understand people experience a mixture of circumstances ranging from joys to challenges going on at any time. That's normal. It's called being "human," and no set of rules or created structure can ever eliminate a person's humanity. It just can't. However, this truth doesn't stop senior leadership, and especially HR, from trying to come up with enough controls to beat the child out of employees and ensure they remain focused as workers.

This has to change. We need to embrace the fact that people are messy . . . and wonderful.

Every single person should have "messy and wonderful" written into their job description. If we acknowledge this is the reality of people, I think organizational cultures would sigh and relax. Far too many people who go to work are stressed and uptight. Much of this is caused by the company's structure itself. Think of how much of your day is spent in trying to keep people in line rather than expecting them to perform.

What would a company look like if employees were given the freedom to express their individuality? It's a beautiful thing to envision. You'd see the unique array of people come to life. Diversity and inclusion would be a natural reality instead of a trumped-up program. Using this approach to your culture doesn't take away from your company's past. If you recognize that the people who brought you this far were able to express their individuality in the first place, you will be able to celebrate who you've been, who you currently are, and who you hope to be.

The one year old who relished being covered in cake and frosting is inside every person who works in your company. The key is to take the steps needed to foster a person's messiness in a productive and constructive way. This is tougher than it sounds because you need to drop the approach of practicing HR collectively. The "one size fits all" initiatives need to be thrown to the side. Instead, build each person up daily so they can rise, fall, fail, and succeed. Give up the control you never had in the first place and teach others who manage people they need to do likewise.

Once you help people become comfortable with a mishmash of individuality coming together as an intricate mosaic, you can identify points of resistance and work with those involved. Take the approach of listening and coach them up to attempt to break through the resistance. This takes an intentional effort from human resources, senior leadership, and people managers. For messy and wonderful individuality to be the norm, these people need to commit to working on this type of culture forever. Not kidding. Forever. As long as your company employs people, you'll need to be intentional with them.

When companies take the steps to elevate people for the unique beings they are, the company thrives. It becomes a magnet for people to join, grow, and lead. It's time to get the piece of cake out and put a candle in it. Sing a song, blow out the candles, and wish the joy about to happen becomes the daily experience of every employee at your company!!

CHAPTER 7

THE THEORY OF HR

I'VE ALWAYS BEEN FASCINATED by Albert Einstein. I've read about his life and his unique way of looking at the universe. It seems like he could be in the same room as others, and he'd see something that was invisible to them. He followed his instincts and was driven to press the limits of his knowledge as well as the boundaries of physics. His theories revolutionized the world, and his impact is still felt to this day as we continue to explore the outer limits of science. People like Einstein deserve our admiration because they have created or discovered ideas and concepts to stretch how we look at the world around us.

It's funny that when we think of areas that deserve expansive thought, the hard sciences come to mind first. People buy into this idea because we can see screens or giant dry erase boards filled with numbers, letters, and symbols, and we may not understand anything that is being written down, but we nod our head in agreement because people far more intelligent than us were able to express themselves in this scientific way. Financial modeling and big data analysis also get the obligatory ooh's and aah's. The math and algorithms are so massive, they seem to crash over us like a giant wave. Every HR professional knows they're supposed to embrace these trends, but few of us truly understand them. Areas that involve in-depth thinking and analysis are incredibly valuable and needed. They often represent the leading edge of new metrics, standards, and benchmarks people can use to measure how they are or aren't performing.

In reflecting on all the numbers swirling around along with the new realities of artificial intelligence and machine learning, one significant aspect of the world of work seems to be overlooked . . . people.

Now, before the futurists, "influencers," and blue-sky theorists raise their objections, hear me out. Business today is not much different than it ever has been throughout history because the focus and attention is on results. When you attend any business meeting, results are the lead driver of most agenda items and discussions. It's understandable because numbers don't talk back and aren't filled with emotions. Numbers fill the endless slides of spreadsheets and P&L monthly statements. When you look around the room, people struggle to get through this constant barrage. They may chime in with some context if pressed, but most people see the sea of digits presented and hope everyone agrees so they can move the meeting along. Once numbers are done being reviewed, new numbers are presented to "move us forward" to the next time period until people gather again.

Results have such a hold on organizations that they force strategic plans, three- to five-year goals, and all performance metrics. Anything not girded and reinforced by numbers is met with doubt and skepticism. It's interesting that very little context is ever asked for when numbers are presented. People rarely question the validity of the information presented. If someone has the courage to press and ask for context around the data, they are dismissed as someone who just doesn't "get it."

I tend to press, and I would encourage others to do so as well. I understand the value of data, analytics, and metrics, and I also acknowledge they are needed to give people a picture of how things were doing (past tense). You see, that's one factor that is never questioned when it comes to an organization that leads from results. Results lag. The activity that generated the work and production of the product or service the company engages in has to be in some form of completion for results to exist. They can't lead because they're history. They are a "result"—an end product.

Over the past year I began meeting with the General Managers of our locations. They are fantastic people and hard workers. I was tasked by my boss to come up with a method of developing our GMs. The reasoning behind this was that our GMs are the focal point of leadership, communication, and culture for our restaurants. When we started these development gatherings, I could sense the skepticism entering the room. I have a good relationship with the GMs because I have made sure to take time to visit each of them at their location to check in with them. My visits are more often temperature checks than some set agenda that lists more and more tasks to add to their already full day.

When we gathered at our Learning Center, I opened the meeting asking everyone how they were doing. Then I sat quietly waiting for responses. It took a few minutes because even though I had a relationship with each of them, any time you're in a group setting, it's harder to openly share. People aren't sure of the norms yet or the environment, tone or intention of the meeting. These great folks have sat through their share of meetings over the years. Their experience has been primarily one of being told they have the company's support (and they do), but then we jump straight into numbers, reports, and tasks. So, when I asked how they were doing, the silence was more out of surprise because they wondered when we were going to get to the normal meeting pattern to which they were accustomed.

Nope. I just sat there.

I didn't have any numbers, reports, or tasks. The only materials I had were three flip charts and some colored markers. No computer. No power point slides. Just me and them. The silence was awkward, and I wanted to jump in to get things moving, but I waited. A few of the more extroverted GMs started sharing when they sensed it was safe, and that broke the ice. I even resisted the HR standard "go to" of having a "get to know you" fun ice breaker. I wanted them to understand that this forum was going to be their time. They were going to have the opportunity to break away from their day-to-day job and have someone listen to them.

I shared that I envisioned a format where I was going to be a facilitator. I'd have some probing questions and areas I'd like to have us discuss, but the majority of our time together was going to be them talking and me taking notes on their ideas, input, challenges, and obstacles. This whole concept was foreign to them because their experience of these types of gatherings usually comprised of reviewing the numbers and results of their store's performance and then asking them how they could improve those numbers and results. To have a chance to just share, vent and express their thoughts was different because they didn't usually feel they had this type of audience. The hectic pace of every day rarely allowed any time for reflection, let alone relaxation.

We spent the rest of the first time together developing ground rules and a schedule for future development meetings. I dismissed everyone and sat in the Learning Center reflecting on how this alternative form of meeting went. I was positive, but I was biased. I told the GMs I was going to visit each of their stores between development meetings to ask their opinion on this meeting approach one-on-one. I wanted to give them the chance to talk in their normal workspace and without a group of peers around. I did this and took their responses to prepare for our next time together.

When we next met, we started with donuts (as you should), coffee, water, and soda, and the opening question, "So, how's everyone doing?" This time people chimed in quickly and shared a variety of stories. Some were long and descriptive, and some were concise. Conversations were now occurring more naturally, and I felt it was time to take the next step.

> "I really appreciate you all coming again, and I enjoyed meeting with you in your stores. After talking to you, I wanted to ask you a question. How much of your day, percentage wise, is spent on people or people-related issues? That could be with your team members or your guests."

Quick note: We call our employees "team members" and the folks who visit our restaurants "guests." Back to the story . . .

One manager said, "Most of my day involves people. I think almost my entire day." Several other managers agreed.

"What percentage of your day?" I asked.

Another manager replied, "Ninety percent." One other manager scoffed. "Must be a light day!! I'd say that ninety-five percent is tied to people."

On one of the flip charts I wrote "90% to 95% of day spent on people."

"Great," I said, "So, what do we ask you to focus on from the corporate side of the business?"

"Results!!" someone quickly shouted. "It's all about the numbers. It's all we hear from you guys.

I wrote the words, "Focus on results," on the same flip chart under the percentages.

"Okay. Fair enough. Do we ask you to focus on anything else?" I asked.

"Yes. We get audited on our processes and how we are doing using them. It usually isn't positive. We have so many of them to follow," shared another GM.

I wrote down, "Focus on processes."

"Great. This works, and this is what I see as well," I replied. "To make sure I have this right, we ask you to focus on results and processes. Is that it?" There were several resounding yeses shared around the room.

"And where to you spend the majority of time during your day?" I asked knowingly.

"We told you. On people."

I looked at the flip charts and said, "Okay, let me try this out and show you what I hear visually." I could see the eye rolls from these solid operations pros wondering what the HR guy was doing. I wasn't discouraged. I drew two circles connected by an equals sign:

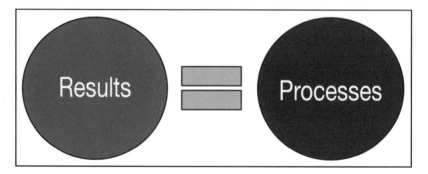

"Does this picture capture how you feel when you communicate with the folks from corporate? 'Here are the results you have, or are expected to achieve, and here are the processes you should follow in order to hit these numbers.' Sound familiar?"

The room was filled with agreement once more. We took a few minutes to share how people felt when they were presented with only these two factors. The answers ranged from frustration to acceptance. The group wanted to have processes and benchmarks. They wanted to have something to strive for because they wanted to have definition as well as an understanding of how the company measured performance and success. It was a rich conversation.

Then I asked, "But what's missing?"

The GMs answered knowingly this time and saw where I was going, "People."

"Exactly," I responded. "Let me show you another formula I'd like you to review and consider." This time I added another circle and a plus sign.

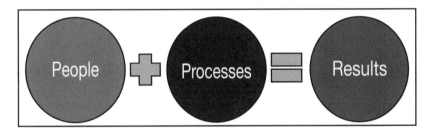

"How about this picture instead? Doesn't this capture how work really exists for all of us? If you work with your people using solid processes, you get better results. You can't ignore the people because that is where most of your time is already being spent."

The GMs liked the formula. Now, no formula can be accepted just because it's written on some flip chart. It needed to be tested. So, I gave the GMs an assignment to wrap up the meeting to try until they came back again next month. I challenged them to intentionally say "Hello" to every single team member and thank them for coming to work every day for thirty days. Every person. Every shift. Every day. They all agreed in principal, and we left for the day.

The next month when we met after asking how everyone was doing, I asked how many of them completed the assignment from the prior meeting. Only half of them had. I didn't get mad or write people up with some form of draconian disciplinary action because they didn't participate. I asked the ones who had done the assignment what they experienced.

I could hardly contain them. They shared that they enjoyed their shifts more and so did their team members. At first, the team members wondered what was going on and some were skeptical about this behavior. It didn't take long for them to eagerly wait to be greeted, and they appreciated being thanked for coming in. Every single one of the stories was positive. Every single one. We had another hour and a half of the development meeting, and I gave the GMs the same assignment for another thirty days. The next month, more of them had participated. Now, after over a year of meeting together, most of them are continuing this behavior.

Yes, it's simple. Yes, I know it doesn't come close to encompassing what happens during a day of business. I don't pretend to think this simple assignment is the entire answer to their develop-ment. It's only the beginning. We've been adding more and more building blocks that are "people first." We are moving towards the processes and then we are going to be mea-suring the results. Like any good scientific method, we'll adjust and tweak where we need to in order to keep driving positive and welcoming behavior.

> **This is the theory of HR, and business, honestly. People plus Processes equals Results.**

This is the theory of HR, and business, honestly. People plus Processes equals Results.

It works every time. If you have a poor view of people, you will experience poorer results than you had hoped for, regardless of solid processes. If you have great people approaches and solid people managers, but your processes are weak, then your results will suffer again. All three factors are needed to exist in harmony.

Too much push or pull from one factor or another will result in an imbalance.

If you want to challenge this, ask your people what they spend the majority of their time on daily. It's people. We aren't complaining about how processes are failing. We personalize the situations and talk about the people involved. You see, people and operations have never been separate entities, even though organizations treat them as if they are. They are intermingled and entwined in such a dense web that they can't exist without one another.

HR take note!! You can lead in the movement to introduce this theory within your four walls. It will bring clarity in a way you haven't seen so far. You can apply it to any situation in any department and at any level of the company. You will experience detractors and doubters along the way, but you need to stick with the theory and show them that every discussion comes back to people. This formula gives you the flexibility to give more definition to the gray areas in which we live and work, and it allows you to bring balance with an approach that will work more often than not. People first. Processes second. And results where they always have been, as results.

CHAPTER 8

CREDIBILITY IS EARNED, TRUST IS GIVEN

ONE OF THE HIGHLIGHTS of my professional career has been the HR Roundtable. I have facilitated a group of professionals for over twenty years, and each month we gather together in person to tackle a hot topic affecting business and HR. The forum is exciting and full of energy. When I began as facilitator, we averaged between 15 to 20 people attending each month. Now we average around 125 to 130 people attending monthly. It's so fun!!

Each time we get together, I pose three questions and the large mass of people break into small groups to discuss each question. After a short period of time, we reconvene and share what was shared in the small breakouts. Inevitably one response comes up every month. Fear.

The answer "fear" takes on many shapes and forms depending on the topic and the question which were being discussed. However, some type of fear is shared at every roundtable. Whenever I hear the word fear mentioned in an organizational context, I must take it to heart, regardless if it's real or perceived. It's real to the people who feel it, experience it, or sense its existence. Whenever I've pressed the respondents about the cause of these fears, the answer is consistent. The cause they give is that trust in the person or people involved is gone. The actions which took place or continue to occur make people cautious and fearful. Each interaction is awkward and uncomfortable, and people are distrustful any productive outcome will happen.

The loss of trust can cripple relationships between people professionally and personally. If trust dissipates, erodes, or disappears, it's nearly impossible to get those involved to effectively work together again. Every person can share countless examples of when they've lost trust in someone. Honestly, we should include ourselves in these stories because we've all lost the trust of others. No one is excluded from this difficult reality when it comes to working with other people.

Since we've been burnt by others at work, we put up our defenses and take the posture that "trust" must be earned. We have some imaginary gauntlet that people must go through before we will give them our trust. When you ask for what it will take to attain this mythical destination, you're given a mixed bag of responses and tasks, which are never the same. The way to earn trust is never defined the same by any two people. As you add to the number of people with whom you interact on a regular basis, this gauntlet grows exponentially until it is honestly not attainable. You may reach a certain level of trust with a few very close coworkers after enough time and trials, but trust can be destroyed within one poor decision or one harsh word.

How in the world can we ever achieve trust when there is no one pathway? I guess we'll just continue to live in a constant state of uncertainty, fear, and disappointment. This sounds like a culture someone would want to join and contribute toward. Unending fear, distrust, and acrimony *must* be the features that make up these Employers of Choice. Who wouldn't be attracted to a company with such an attractive culture of mistrust?

Trust can't be earned. It can't. People will screw it up. They can't help it. We all disappoint each other and fail. It's a significant aspect of being human. You can trust that you'll fail (Sorry for the pun), but it's a given. You can count on this to occur on a regular basis for a myriad of reasons, which will constantly shift and change. Sounds encouraging, doesn't it?

It's time for HR to rewrite the textbook on trust.

It's time for HR to rewrite the textbook on trust. There is a way to alleviate fear and provide a healthy, constructive environment and culture where people can work together, faults and all.

Trust has to be given first.

Whenever two people get together, trust has to be extended to each person initially, and it needs be unconditional. This approach runs counter to human history and the expectation of people today. That's okay. It's great to go against the flow of what people expect. Leaders look for ways to turn the tide and change the direction and behavior of people. They don't force people into marching in step down the same paths hoping that things will change.

Trust can't be earned, but credibility can. Credibility is earned based on the behavior of each person on their own, which is all that can really be directed and controlled. People can't control anything in their day other than their thoughts, actions, words, and reactions. Every other aspect of a person's day is circumstantial at best. It's not surprising workers feel out of sorts during their day because they not only have life going on, they're trying to maneuver through a trust gauntlet.

HR should take the lead when it comes to building credibility. This isn't some program or ten-week training program that follows a set list of do's and don'ts. Credibility is earned in how you approach and treat others. It's modeled by your daily activity and interactions. It especially is gauged by what you say about others. You have a choice, just like every other human, to lift people up through your words or to tear them down. There is no middle ground.

The words we use between, and about, each other carry immeasurable weight and meaning. If you step back and evaluate the employee relations issues you have at your company, you'll find poorly used words at the crux of every situation. Those words destroy a person's credibility and trust. The challenge with credibility when it comes to the words we use to describe people and situations is that emotion will override any sense of logic. How many times have phrases been blurted out only for people to wish they had never shared what was said?

The reason credibility needs to be earned before it can be modeled and taught to others is simple. Credibility can't be self-proclaimed. It has to be visible and confirmed by others. Once credibility is established, the hardest step presents itself. You must be consistent in how you act and interact with others. It never stops. You have to be conscious of how you treat others and do your best to be consistent because you will stumble and fall. The difference between losing credibility and losing trust is that when you fail, you must acknowledge the failure and own it. This can't be some false pretense just to get out of the uncomfortable place you're in. Own it. Be a leader and say why and how you failed and what you plan to do going forward.

There's a second part to owning your failures. Show grace to others when they fail you. Again, this needs to be genuine and not some act you put on in front of the hurt parties only to gossip about people when they're out of earshot. Empathy is missing in today's HR and organizations. We want someone to fry for failure at the same time we proclaim that it's "okay" to miss the mark because that's how people learn. This is one of the largest mixed messages existing in today's workplace.

HR has to stop thinking that trust and credibility are the responsibility of senior leadership only. We have the opportunity to show others the potential of making credibility a reality by choosing to step into this area intentionally. Isn't it time we plant the seeds of credibility? We can establish credibility through our actions. We need to be accountable for our communication, our encouragement, and our commitments to the work for which we are responsible. Just imagine what your workplace would be like when trust is given and credibility is earned. This needs to be our standard and the baseline from which the profession exists without question.

Evaluate where you stand as a credible resource before you reach out to others. This isn't a platform for you to be preachy and point fingers. It's an opportunity to be the north star of your organization by being credible yourself first. Once you know this is the case, set the expectation of credibility with your department if you're fortunate enough to have people who report to you. If you're an HR department of one, then reach out to those whom you work with the most and make sure they are your credible "team." Then, and only then, can you make this behavior the foundation for other departments, people managers and senior leadership.

It's time to alleviate organizational fears by taking the steps needed to be the credible person you were meant to be. When this happens, you will be more comfortable in your role and your ability to make a sustainable difference in the lives of others. This, in turn, will completely reshape your company to become a phenomenal workplace as a reality and not an aspiration.

CHAPTER 9

USE A KALEIDOSCOPE

I'M SOMEONE WHO LOVES TOYS. I always have since I was a kid. In fact, my wife and kids (now adults) have an easy time during the holidays or birthdays because they get me things to play with. When you go out to shop for someone knowing what you purchase will bring them joy, a giant smile, and a hearty belly laugh, it makes shopping an adventure and not a chore. I'm not kidding.

My office, and the basement of my home, are filled with puzzles, lava lamps, tie-dyed stuffed llamas, a KISS Pez set in full make-up, and a Harry Potter wizarding chess set just to name a few. They recently gave me a rock legend paper doll book where you create miniature versions of people who shaped the world of rock 'n' roll. It will be a thrill to assemble this set of icons. But I digress . . .

You see, it's easy for someone to lose themselves when they connect with something that fills their passion bucket. They would rather spend their time and focus with their passions than anything else in front of them.

What would companies look like if that passion was reflected and lived out by our employees and people managers? What if every time you interacted with any other person in the company you lost yourself because both you and others were consumed with the joy of working together? It's such a foreign concept to us that we don't even think this level of genuine enjoyment is even possible.

Our experience is more encompassed with daily griping and complaining about coworkers. This constant flow of disdain isn't limited to certain levels of roles in companies. Everyone talks about others in more negative terms than positive ones. Don't believe me? Try this experiment on an upcoming Monday. Go to work and greet those you normally greet. Don't alter your normal pattern. Have regular conversations, and then at lunch take out a piece of paper and recall any conversation you had. See how much of those interactions involved comments about others and how they fell short of what they were supposed to do. See how much of your paper is filled up with these negative conversations which you haven't seen as negative at all in the past. You, and I, have become accustomed to this being how we talk at work.

Isn't it ironic that what companies tout as the most valuable aspect of their organization is rarely seen in a positive light? This is a facet of HR I didn't want to accept. If you spend the majority of your day surrounded by negative conversations, then you will rarely see all the fantastic, positive work being accomplished daily.

I wasn't sure how to break through this cloudy, muddled, dark standard until I remembered a response I once received from a candidate after an interview. I was working for an engineering and architectural consulting firm, and we were looking to add a Director of Marketing. We had never had someone whose sole focus was marketing to our clients to develop future business opportunities on an on-going basis. We had relied on word of mouth and the quality of our work as the vehicle to secure continued sales. This had run its course, and we needed to add talent to help us grow and thrive. We had interviewed several folks for the role, and many were qualified. However, one person responded to his interview in such a way that distinguished him from anyone else who we had met.

After his second interview, he sent me a box. I was curious to see what was in this box but confused why I would receive such an unusual thank-you after an interview. I eagerly opened the package and saw a kaleidoscope. A note was wrapped around the multi-colored tin tube. It said, "Steve, you asked for someone who would look at business and marketing in a different way. I'm that person and I look forward to working with you one day soon." I was floored!! I grabbed the package and ran out to my boss, who had also received a kaleidoscope. It turned out this candidate sent four of these wonderful old-fashioned toys to the four of us who had interviewed him. He was offered the job that day, and he accepted.

This kaleidoscope gave me an idea of how to address how we look at people in my current company. It would be risky because the great people I work with are very hands-on folks who are much more comfortable talking about tasks and processes than receiving a toy. I knew I couldn't just give everyone a kaleidoscope because it would be seen as an odd silly HR trick. Since I was going old school with my surprise give away, I pulled out my other antique training method—my trusty flip chart.

I stood before our managers in a meeting where I was given twenty minutes to help them reflect on how they viewed the people they worked with. The meeting was a launch for a new program intended to define and frame our overall company culture. I knew this would be a challenge because we didn't have a ton of time for an interactive session, which I'm far more comfortable leading. We had spent over an hour laying out the new program, which was solid, but was delivered in a traditional teacher/student lecture approach. When I stood up in front of the group, I wanted to change the tone and the level of feedback and involvement.

I wrote the word "EMPLOYEES" in all caps along the top of the blank flip chart page. I turned to the managers and posed the question, "When you think of employees, how would you describe them?" This was the spark to the gasoline I was sure was quietly flowing through each person present.

"They're lazy," stated one manager. There were several grunts of acknowledgement.

"Cool," I responded. "What else?

I was careful not to correct this response and give the manager the sugar-coated corporate response she was used to receiving.

"They don't know their jobs." "They don't listen or show up on time." "They're unreliable."

The answers became more and more visceral and emotional. You could sense that the answers were heading toward a crescendo. The more responses I received, the more I egged them on. "Get it out," I encouraged. "Let me know how you feel. It's okay and I want to hear it all."

The page continued to fill with negative response after negative response until someone finally shouted out, "They're a pain in the ass!!"

Everyone nodded in agreement and giggled that they were "allowed" to vent so freely. This hadn't been their experience in past meetings. I laughed as well because the exercise was freeing and fun. That's right. The head of HR for the entire company liked hearing the way people were viewed even though it was negative because it was finally *honest*!! The same descriptors I knew were flying around the location during the typical business day were now presented openly and without judgement.

The next step threw the room for a loop and was the risky part of this experiment. I matched the heightened level of emotions and excitement and said, "Okay, let me recap. According to you, employees are lazy, stupid, full of drama, unreliable and . . . a pain in the ass!!" The managers howled back, "YES!!!!"

Then I asked, "Cool. So, who in the room is an employee?" and I raised my hand to see who else would jump in. All of their hands shot up and then quickly back down. "You jerk," I heard someone mumble. I turned back to the flip chart and added the word, "Jerk."

The room that had just been filled with a fervor of pent-up feelings finally coming out fell ominously silent. I jumped in while the shock was still setting in and explained we have all lost sight of how awesome employees are. We get caught up in the negative behavior that a few people exhibit, so we conclude every person must be awful. I shared that it's easy to fall into the trap of viewing others poorly. I also shared how it was something that I had to work on every day so I didn't do the same thing. I showed them we had something in common. I'm also someone surrounded by people, and conversations about behavior take up my entire workday.

I reached into my duffel bag I had hidden off to the side during the flip chart word association exercise and pulled out kaleidoscopes and gave one to each manager. Like most trainers would, I instantly jumped into talking again to make my point around why everyone was getting a kaleidoscope. No one listened because I had missed what was happening right in front of me.

Instead of sitting dutifully to my incredibly insightful context about people and our differences, the managers all pointed their new toy up to the lights and looked through them. Then they slowly turned the ends of their kaleidoscope to see the beautiful colored patterns change with each rotation. They all started to chatter and reminisce about having a kaleidoscope when they were young. They noted they hadn't seen them in years and a few of the younger managers had to be taught how to use the toy because they had never seen one. They played for several minutes, and it was beautiful. That break in their day to play was more meaningful than jumping straight into my poignant explanation.

After everyone put their kaleidoscope down, one manager asked, "Can we keep them?"

I said, "Absolutely." Then I hit them with my prepared point. "Everyone we work with and meet in life is different. We lose sight of this fact and we forget that each one of them brings a unique perspective and talent to work. I want you to keep the kaleidoscopes because from now on, I want you to look at employees differently. I want you to picture them as the colorful, bright, and constantly moving shapes you see when you point your kaleidoscope to the light."

Then, I sat back down. That was what I had wanted to communicate and accomplish. I wanted to shift the mindset of our great people managers. It was a valiant start and you can see kaleidoscopes in restaurant offices to this day.

If you want to take the lead in diversity and inclusion in your organization HR, then buy yourself a kaleidoscope as a reminder. We need to come to understand that diversity exists and always has. It's not a program or initiative. It's a fact. You can't add to it. You can recognize and embrace diversity and then work towards inclusion. However, it starts with how you, and others, view people.

Buy some kaleidoscopes for the people of your organization. Conduct this exercise and then give them a toy to be a visual reminder of the great mosaic we're a part of on a regular basis. Just remember that when you pass them out, give people time to play and rekindle the joy of what toys offer. Remember the kid inside of every employee. It's a joy that will ensure an on-going energy and sense of life throughout your culture.

CHAPTER 10

LISTEN TO THE MUSIC

HOW OLD ARE YOU? Don't worry, I'm the head of human resources and I'm allowed to ask you. I need to know so I can make wild generalizations about you because of the generation you're from. On top of that, I'm going to lump you into an entire group of others who are in your age range so I can box you in to stereotypes sure to be present because I can confirm them from your birth certificate.

Sounds ridiculous and incredibly discriminatory doesn't it? It is. And, shamefully, it's supported and pursued by companies, human resource professionals, and an endless list of conference speakers and authors. Equally disheartening is that few people push back against this. We all seem comfortable with blocking people into age segments. Once the segmentation occurs, we go so far as to predict how someone will perform or interact solely based on their age. There are entire purchasing and marketing campaigns based on breaking people into their generations.

Quick question. When did companies start having people from various generations work together in the same work environment? The answer is: Whenever work began. Now, unless you were around at the dawn of work, you can't dispute this.

When we split people up because of age, we go one dreadful step further. We focus on generational differences instead of a person's strengths. When we list the differences, we inevitably start comparing what we don't like about those differences. This leads to complaining and then you're on a path that only gets more negative. It isn't pretty and could end up even becoming discriminatory.

The unfortunate generational divide that keeps being perpetuated ate at my core. I remember when my father would tell me how hard his generation worked and that my generation was made up of nothing but slackers who didn't value work the way his generation did. He was one of those fathers who swore he began working in earnest when he was either two or three years old because everyone had to carry their weight on the farm. They couldn't afford for anyone to not be a contributor. I remember rolling my eyes and shrugging any time I got the "you don't know how hard we had it" speech.

As a quick point of reference, I'm technically a baby boomer by age, but I have always identified with Generation X. I only use this break to give you the labels I hope to destroy in just a few paragraphs.

One of the amazing and fortunate parts of my professional career is that I've been able to be a speaker at HR conferences. I have always enjoyed the opportunity to get in front of my peers and share thoughts, concepts, ideas, and stories. Stepping onto a stage gives me deep fulfillment, but I never take it for granted. It's something I cherish, and I hope people learn something they can take away and apply in their roles at work.

I felt I needed to confront this age divide head-on and decided to do that in front of large groups at HR conferences. As I was in the middle of a presentation, I would ask for a volunteer from the audience. The extroverts attending instantly shot their hands up for the chance to be in front of the crowd, but I never chose a fellow extrovert for a reason. I would scan the attendees and look for the youngest possible person. I'd invite them to join me and ask everyone to applaud for the "willing" volunteer as they came forward. As they sheepishly join me, I'm sure they think I'm going to perform some humiliating task which makes me shine while they look foolish. That's not the case, but I can understand the anxiety because I've seen far too many other speakers do this. Instead, I want to get their input and opinion.

I reach behind the table filled with toys and trinkets from my office that always appears at my presentations and grab a large white cardboard square. I ask my volunteer what they think this object is. Over the years, I've received a variety of answers which are pretty creative, but recently people have been reintroduced to this marvel of communication. The big square I'm holding is the cover for a record album. The one that travels with me is the essential, classic *White Album* by the Beatles. This album is a true treasure of mine because I purchased it a record store called Haffa's during my college years at Ohio University. Haffa was an honest-to-goodness long-haired, tie-dyed hippie who spoke in terms and phrases dripping with coolness. Another reason the album is such a treasure is this copy was printed on white vinyl versus the traditional black vinyl used for records. It was also recorded and produced on The Beatles' own Apple Records brand.

I explain to the audience and my volunteer that when I showed the disc to my kids and asked them what they thought it was, they gave me answers like "a plate" and "a Frisbee." I told them it was something far more interesting and asked them to sit in front of my turntable and speakers from my fully geeked-out sound system. I dropped the needle on the edge of the rotating white disc and the first sound emitted from the massive speakers of my stereo system was a screeching jet engine and a guitar riff underpinned with some drums as "Back in the U.S.S.R." started to play. "There's music on that thing?" my daughter squealed. They had never heard a record play before.

I get back to my volunteer and pull out a much smaller rectangle with writing scrawled all over the label in my handwriting. "How about this? Do you know what this is?"

Almost every time, my helper tells me it's a cassette. I tell the audience this is my copy of the same *White Album* I recorded so I could take the music with me and play it in my car or my Sony Walkman. The third square I pull out is smaller than the record album and bigger than the cassette. "That's a CD," they blurt out because they've caught on to the analogy I'm using.

I agree and show them the CD copied the album by putting the double album on two shiny discs. The next rectangle is gray with a big circle on its face. "That's an iPod." They're into this now and forget they're on stage because they've become more comfortable. I congratulate them for recognizing the iPod and explain the same fabulous Beatles tunes are on this little piece of technology along with over 12,000 other songs because I'm a music freak.

The final rectangle I pull out is my iPhone, and I don't ask them what it is because *everyone* has a phone, which really is a computer far more than it is a phone these days. I then pull up a streaming service and I start playing my favorite Beatles song ever, "Blackbird."

I close by telling the volunteer and the entire audience that the various methods of music represent the generations in the workplace. Even though each one is different, the music is still the same.

I thank my able assistant and get the group to offer up one more round of applause. After they take their seat, I deliver the point of the whole trip through the many types of delivering music.

"What would our companies be like if we focused on the music instead of the different ways it's delivered? It is way past time for us to change the message of splitting people up because of the generation when they happened to be born."

This message and call to action are far more than some schtick to get people's attention during an HR conference presentation. HR should never participate, condone, or allow genera-tional separation in their organization. It's unthink-able to me that we would thwart discrimination of all other kinds and yet fall into this rut of stereotyping. We should do all we can to eliminate labels and segmentation.

> **We should do all we can to eliminate labels and segmentation.**

People are different ages. You can't change or influence this fact. Our age difference is just one of the countless differences that make each human unique. Instead of pointing out differences, we should leverage them and look at the strengths that these char-acteristics offer. If you have an older employee who has several years of tenure under their belt, what could you learn from their experiences? If you have someone new to the workforce, what if you asked them to look at their role and the organization with a set of new eyes? You can come up with more and more examples of ways to incorporate the unique perspectives of your people.

HR needs to charge against this form of discrimination with the same fervor we give toward any appearance of discrimination. We should stand up to others who use separatist language, behavior, and actions and coach them on what they're doing. Take the time to teach others that the music is the same. Allow people to play their vinyl, cassette, CD, iPod, or streaming platform. You can even allow the random 8-track tape in if someone happens to still use those. They all can come together just as we should as people. We need to do this now because I'm sure the next way to share music is on the horizon. Let's include each new generation that's coming and teach others how to do this for years and years to come.

CHAPTER 11

SLOW DOWN !!

ONE OF MY FAVORITE SONGS of all time comes from the folk duo Simon & Garfunkel. They penned a song which resonated with the times when it was written in the 1960's, and even more so today. It's the "59th Street Bridge Song," you know the one whose opening line implores listeners to "slow down." Don't worry, you know this.

When I grew up, we called it the "Feelin' Groovy" song, which is actually a part of the original title. The message is simple, but most would consider it unrealistic. Whenever you ask somebody what the rush is in what they're doing, they can't give you a clear answer. The general sentiment is we are so starved for time that every single action of the day must occur with haste. No exceptions. The pressure and pace of life in general feels like a weight that never stops pressing down on our thoughts. The level of stress brought on by this pressure can be insurmountable at times.

As the song states so philosophically, we do move too fast. Expediency is sought after in every aspect of business today. Wherever we can eliminate one second of wasted time, we gain seventeen minutes!! No, that's not true, but the trimming of time for the sake of more speed is given exponential value in companies. I understand we should be efficient and timely. A focus on being the most productive in the most expedient way—with quality—may give you an incredible competitive advantage. The challenge is that we apply this stopwatch pace to all aspects of business, which is neither sustainable nor feasible.

Have you ever watched someone who is an avid walker or runner? They establish a pace that works for them. They know if they are consistent with their pace, then they'll achieve their workout goal. A person who runs a marathon gradually increases the distance they run during training, so they are in the best position to complete the race when it occurs. During this even more grueling period of training, they establish a pace that works for them. When people are involved in this type of activity, no one mirrors the exact pace of any other person. Their end goal is to finish. It may also be to compete with others, but that is only during events and races. Most of their activity is to stay active and work on their well-being.

Work has a pace as well. Like walkers and runners, it isn't the same for any two people who are involved. This tends to frustrate people because we think *everyone* should imitate and match the pace of the alleged leader of any work effort. The difference between walkers, runners, and work is that at work the only speed recognized and rewarded is breakneck speed. There is also a fear, which is completely unfounded, that if a group of workers slow down in any meaningful way, failure is assured.

We talk about employees who are more and more disengaged in the workplace today. I'm sure there are many factors that contribute to disengagement, but I haven't heard people talk about the unreasonable pace of work. I don't have data to support this other than observational experience. Whenever I'm out with our employees, the first emotion that hits me after I greet them is utter exasperation. If they could be in running shorts, it would fit how spent they feel on a daily basis. Some of this rushing around may be needed due to the volume of work in front of them. However, even when a natural break happens during their day, the rush continues. It never fades, and this is concerning.

How can organizations hope to move forward in any tangible manner if everyone is exhausted all the time?

How can organizations hope to move forward in any tangible manner if everyone is exhausted all the time? Have you ever gone to a meeting and you hear audible, heavy sighs as each person takes their seat around the table? Are you the one making the loud exhale?

HR can jump in to tackle the "race" and slow it to a "pace." If this is done well, you will add significant value to the work that needs to be performed. There is risk in stating people should slow down because the nature of companies for decades will revolt against you as an adversary. You will face pushback and ridicule from folks who will say there's no room for this nonsense. They'll state there just isn't "time" for anyone to slow down, and they will use data to prove their point.

This is where you need to pull out *your* formula and remind them that:

People + Processes = Results

Processes are based on efficiency and are meant to drive down time and waste. Again, those are valuable attributes, but with this mindset, you eliminate any human variation which is present whether you want it to be or not.

One day I was out visiting one of our pizzerias, which is one of the most favorite aspects of my job. Any time I can be out among our team members, my bucket is filled. If you've never been in a restaurant's kitchen, it's a symphony of constant movement. The movement accelerates and slows in response to the orders coming through on the printed tickets. Our locations move from a steady to a frenetic pace within moments. I was walking through one of our kitchens and I saw one of our cooks training a new team member on how to make a pizza.

They were going through the steps rapidly because they were familiar with the process and it was second nature to them. They didn't even look up to see if the trainee was paying attention. They were so adept that it took mere seconds to put together a beautiful creation, which was easily put onto a conveyor to go through the oven. The training cook said, "Okay, your turn," and the trainee fumbled around. They tried to repeat what was just shown to them, and they failed. The trainer grunted, "Here!" and grabbed the partially created pizza and whipped out another perfect pie to go into the over. "Try again," he chided.

I could see a chance to tip the apple cart a bit. I stepped in and said, "I see the problem here."

"Who are you?" asked the trainee. "Oh, that's Steve, the HR guy. Don't worry about him," replied the trainer.

"No, seriously. I see what's wrong here." I pointed to the next clean dough sitting on the prep table. "Your dough's upside down."

"What?" they both replied in astonishment.

"It is. Look." I picked up the dough and flipped it over. It looked exactly the same as the other side. (Please note: we use flash frozen doughs so it isn't hard to do this.)

The trainer was catching on to what I was doing. "He's just some dude from the corporate office. He doesn't do *real* work. I know what I'm doing. Flip the dough back over the way it was." The frightened newbie complied and flipped the dough over once again.

"I don't think you understand who I am," looking at his nametag, "David. I have the power to hire and fire here at the company. It's upside down. Listen to me and flip it back over." He complied becoming even more fearful and confused.

Our trainer said, "Steve's harmless and he doesn't even know how to make a pizza himself!! He's in human resources. Trust me. Turn the dough back over." David tentatively looked at me to see if it was okay, making sure this wasn't the last dough he ever touched. I nodded that it was okay, and he flipped it over one final time.

I said, "I'll let this one slide. But, if I were you Tom, I'd slow down and show David how to make pizza so he can become as good at it as you are." We all laughed. David did so a bit nervously, but Tom did slow down and took his time in teaching David his craft.

I came back a few weeks later to see how David was doing and he was able to make pizzas quickly and correctly while keeping up with the tickets that kept printing like a waterfall on a busy Friday night shift. He smiled and greeted me when I walked through, and so did Tom. We recounted the upside-down dough experience and laughed again.

I found out later that David became so good he became a trainer of new team members himself. He and Tom would gang up and do the upside-down dough trick on a person's first shift. New team members enjoyed learning from Tom and David, and as a result, they enjoyed their work.

Now, I understand this is one simple story. However, there are processes in your organization where you can step in and slow things down a bit and possibly turn some things upside-down. The time is there. You can take this approach where you see things racing out of control and exasperation setting in. Set the pace. It is far more effective and sustainable.

CHAPTER 12

FOSTER VS. FORCE

I FONDLY REMEMBER attending elementary school. I went to an extremely small rural school for my first three grades and a bigger school for fourth through sixth grade. My favorite activity of the day, like most of the other students, was recess. When the bell would ring proclaiming the end of the period, and all of us would rush to get into a straight, single file line at the door. We were fidgeting with anticipation to be able to rush out into the fresh air to run, skip, squeal, and play. We always thought the teachers were too slow in releasing us to freedom. Little did we know that they looked forward to recess just as much as we did. For them, it was as much of a break from us as it was for us from them.

Behavior out on a playground is fascinating to watch and be a part of. You see kids run headlong to the playground equipment like swings, slides, and teeter totters. Others head to find the various jump ropes or balls that were kept in a large wire basket. Distinct separations occur the moment the single line breaks through to the wide-open blacktop and grassy areas of the playground expanse. Kids quickly seek out their friends so that they can finally talk after being cooped up for what seemed like an eternity during all of the lessons prior to escaping. The groups would most typically break into boys going to some crazy physical activity so they could burn off as much pent-up energy as possible, and the girls would congregate into games where they could talk as well as be active.

Inevitably, someone would shout out that we should pick teams and play a game. That game could be dodgeball, kickball, tag, or kick the can. Whenever someone made the self-proclamation that they were the "captain" and that one of their more assertive peers was the other "captain," the rest of the kids would gather in some mass opposite of the new "leaders." Then the painful, and rapid, choosing of teams occurred because teams had to be formed quickly so everyone could play for the maximum amount of time before heading back to desks and books. Some kids reveled in the picking of teams while others dreaded it. This was because the self-appointed captains chose their friends first regardless of any measure of skill. If they liked you, you were picked. After the initial few who were always chosen early, the rest of the kids who wanted to play stared longingly, thinking about two things. One was that they wanted to be chosen, and second, they didn't want to be the last kid who was "picked" but whom no one truly wanted on their team.

The teams would run to the activity of the day, and countless "rules" that were never equally applied were shouted out before the game commenced. The game would be played among several arguments of something being unfair because the competition level was so heightened. No one ever "won," but one team would loudly proclaim victory as the bell to return to class rang and the teachers beckoned everyone back into a straight line to head back to the next lesson.

I learned a ton from recess about myself because I was someone who held most of the roles. I started out as the kid who was the last to be chosen because I didn't have many friends established. After some time, I got close to a few of the kids who were usually captains and I was picked more quickly. There were even a few times I stepped up and proclaimed myself as captain so I could choose.

Now, I wish I could say that when I had the chance to be the captain that I was benevolent and remembered what it was like to not be chosen. But I didn't. I was just as coarse as the other kids who were captains, choosing who I liked. I'm not proud of that, by the way. It was an opportunity to see how more people could have been included. However, I was young and impetuous. I just wanted to play and wasn't astute enough to think, or care, about the other kids to any meaningful extent.

Doesn't this playground remind you of someplace you go almost every day of the year? You don't get recess now, but the workplace has the same dynamics and behaviors as those days back in elementary school. Teams assemble for both short-term and long-term projects. Can you picture the "captains" that are either self-proclaimed or have positioned themselves in front of senior leadership enough that this is how they're designated? They pick their teams in much the same way kickball teams were chosen when we were young. You have to realize that people will choose those with whom they are most comfortable or compatible. They will rarely choose a teammate who they feel is contrary or will detract from their presumed performance or chemistry.

Teams continue to be formed just as they were on the playground. After people are assigned roles within teams, you should look up to see the people who weren't chosen. They exist now just as they did then. One difference in the workplace is that people are sometimes forced onto teams because they are expected to participate. This builds an instant resentment by the existing "chosen" team members and the person who was shoe-horned in. We are more content with making sure structure exists than we are with the performance of both the team and the individuals who make up the team.

Teams are needed in the workplace. When you get a group of people together, you bring in a myriad of perspectives, viewpoints, ideas, and approaches. Teaming that is crafted and done well can be immensely successful. The question is: Do you have the patience to foster teamwork versus forcing it?

During my career, I've had bosses who wished that people would naturally work together. They hoped that others seeing the greater good and the vision laid out before them would be enough of a spark of interest to draw people together. That would be incredible, and it does exist in pockets throughout organizations, but it is not the norm.

> **Do you have the patience to foster teamwork versus forcing it?**

When leaders bump into two or more people who are hesitant to work together, they will go to the person who is more approachable of those involved. They'll tell the more approachable person that they should reach out and work with the other party. Just "play nice." This forced action fails every time, even if the approachable person makes the effort to connect.

We've forgotten the behavior that was exhibited on the playground. When kids were friends, they were chosen. In work terms this means fostering relationships between the people you want to work together. HR should lift the torch to foster relationships. It would be a far more impactful effort than continuing the practice of doing countless performance reviews to denote how people struggle with each other. If HR would assess the talent of their organization in an objective manner, then they can see where people share commonalities and where differences exist. This doesn't mean that you only build teams that have commonalities. Instead, you should strive to build teams with people whose strengths complement each other.

Base the formation of teams on skills, attributes, characteristics, and diversity. Fight the urge to let teams form based only on friendships because that just continues to allow homogeneous teams. They may all get along, but their work and output will be narrow and reflective of the sameness of each team member. Mix it up. Make sure that you are inclusive because you're aware of the strengths and gaps of the employees of each department of your company. For those who work in massive organizations, use this same approach for the people with whom you interact the most. HR can, and should, be a team builder. That is far more effective than being named the captain because you declared it. Please note that being the team builder doesn't mean you're "in charge" of teams. You have the opportunity to foster the skills needed for others to learn how to be team builders themselves. This can lead to a chain reaction of behavior that will result in productive teams and team members. When people are "chosen" now, there's context and substance. That is the difference that HR can bring to the table.

You have to break the old models of team formation when you move towards fostering and stop forcing. Start small and then scale it up once you start seeing successes. This isn't easy, but leadership was never meant to be easy. Be the catalyst that redefines teamwork and see how your results begin to move the organization forward as well as get the work needed done.

CHAPTER 13

I SEE IT IN YOU

THERE HAS BEEN A MOVEMENT within organizations that I have never been comfortable with. I don't like when we identify people as "high potentials." I understand the intention and the concept that companies want to see if people will grow and develop into people that can take on more responsibility and leadership. Companies should keep their eyes open to see who is performing at a higher level than others. It keeps us mindful of who is more engaged and who is more active. It may not ensure the outcome of employees performing for the long-term, but it certainly does grab our attention.

I'm not against looking for people to advance. Sure, you get people who are shining stars who blast onto the scene and make contributions that may have great impact for a while. You may benefit from this burst of brilliance, and it could have been needed at a certain point in time because things weren't moving. The problem with companies focusing on these shooting stars is that they either fade away or they wait for the next time to build up and explode into visibility once again. My experience with people who have these spurts and shifts is that this is how they most effectively perform. They are honestly content having the space and ability to do this.

Unfortunately, these "stars" get pigeonholed into a leadership box because companies want them to replicate their leaps and chunks of forward progress with others as direct reports. Being a bright, shining star doesn't mean that you will be a successful leader. In fact, it often sputters, and you end up having to address the lack of performance of your once identified high potential. There's no reason to rush and place people in positions of scale and authority because they happen to be more visible and vocal. I think that organizations still subtly couch this labeling and rapid promotions under the mantras of "let the cream rise to the top" or "people need to sink or swim." These are archaic and have rarely worked.

Wouldn't you rather have people grow into roles through development? Everyone has a ceiling. Even the person who exhibits the most promise will hit a ceiling. This isn't right or wrong. It's just a fact. Every human has a certain capacity where they can be filled to the brim and still crush it. Once you surpass that capacity, people start to fail more often. It would be ideal to have all employees performing at their natural capacity. Just like other comparatives mentioned so far in this book, no person has the same capacity as someone else. We need to quit trying to make a cadre of super-performers at each and every level of an organization. It's too hard to define, and it also takes so much continuous effort and energy that you burn people out.

There's a different tactic that you can take when it comes to developing the talent that exists throughout your company. It takes someone who is willing to be an observer. This position of observation will possess more leadership than you think because they have the responsibility of looking for those who may be able to step into larger roles. They see the potential of others and open the doors for them to walk through. Then they are also available to coach, encourage, and correct those whom they identify to make sure they have the best chance to succeed in both the short term and long term.

Janet, a parent at my kids' school, was this type of observer. When my son was going into first grade, he and I went to a meeting after school one night about Cub Scouts. Now, I don't know if you've been to a meeting where parents are expected to jump into leadership roles as volunteers, but this was this type of meeting. I know that these "volunteer" meetings happen in all sorts of organizations from kids' sports teams to civic and religious organizations. Volunteer leaders are needed because they do two things. One, they keep the parents connected and involved and two, they serve as a role model for the kids who are participating.

I just wanted to go and check out what the program had to offer, and I was more curious than anything else. I didn't count on Janet being at the meeting. I was new to this program and since my son was so young, I didn't know any other parents or kids yet. I listened to the presentation and watched the power point slides, which showed boys involved in several activities. The boys were all outside with older scouts playing so the parents could pay attention. Janet introduced the Cub Master and then sat down. I looked at her during the Cub Master's description of the Pack's values, leadership, and structure. They covered the commitment of time for participation for the kids and their parents, and then they make the "ask."

"Well, that's all we had for tonight. If your boys would like to join our Pack, we'd love to have them. We also need Den Leaders so the boys have a place to meet and a group of peers to do scouting with. Who'd like to be a Den Leader?"

As you'd expect, not one hand was lifted. The Cub Master looked a bit forlorn and sighed, but he'd been through this a few years already. He thanked us for coming and hoped that some of the parents would reconsider so that our sons could join and enjoy scouting. At that point, the room came to life as all of the first graders came running back in, dripping with sweat and still full of energy. My son couldn't stop talking about the cool older scouts he met and all of the fun he had while I sat through the PowerPoint slides.

I was glad he was geeked, and I took him by the hand while I gathered up the informational packet we had been given. Then Janet stopped me.

"Is this your son?" she asked knowingly. "I'm Josh!!" he quickly replied.

"Did you have fun tonight, Josh?" Janet asked, again knowingly. "YES!!!!" he shouted. She turned her attention directly to me.

"Wouldn't it be great if Josh had fun like this all the time?"

I squirmed and tried to avoid eye contact, which is not like me at all. "Yeah, that would be great," I said.

"I was watching you tonight. I'm Janet, and you are?"

"Steve."

"Nice to meet you, Steve. I saw that you were interested in what we talked about tonight. What did you like?"

We talked for about five minutes, and I shared that I liked the different activities and it seemed like the other adults who were in the Scout uniforms all seemed engaged and close to each other. I explained that was very appealing.

"I think you should be a Den Leader," she stated. "I mean it. I see it in you. We need leaders who are interested in seeing the boys participate and engage. I think you'd make sure that happens. It would be great to have you join the other leaders."

I was floored by how direct she was. She wasn't forceful or aggressive. She was just decisive.

"Tell you what. I'll give you a few days to think about it. Here's my cell number. Can I get yours?" she asked.

I agreed and gave her my number. In two days, I received a call from Janet. After we exchanged hellos, she said, "How's my next Den Leader doing today?" Again, I was caught off guard, but I wasn't upset. She explained that Dens needed to get formed soon and she'd like to contact the boys who signed up earlier that week to tell them that they had a Den where they could start their scouting journey. She was so inviting and positive that I felt comfortable in saying, "Yes, I'll be the Den Leader."

She was pleased with my response, and she proceeded to tell me the five other boys and dads who were joining me in my Den. She had already told the other families I was going to lead even though I hadn't accepted yet. Her boldness was daunting and intriguing at the same time.

I was glad I stepped into the Den Leader role for my son and for the others who joined us. We had a grand time. After I had been in the Pack for two years, Janet showed up at my house. She didn't call. She just showed up. I had known her now for two years and was used to her doing this type of thing.

"Steve, you got a second?" I knew I couldn't tell her that I had something going on. She had already positioned herself in a way to make sure a conversation was going to occur.

"What's up, Janet?"

"Steve, our Cub Master is going to step down at the end of this school year and I think you should replace him. The scouts in the Pack flock around you and you take a genuine interest in them and their families. I think it would be an easy transition for you. I see you in this role already."

I'm sure you know what happened. I became the Assistant Cub Master for a year and then stepped into the Cub Master role. I still was the Den Leader for our original group of kids, and we added a few others who kept growing with the program. After you go through Cub Scouts, your son has the choice to continue to Boy Scouts. My son and I visited some Troops including one with many of the young men who had been Cub Scouts with Josh. The Scout Master of the troop, Patrick, invited our Den to come camping with the troop. We went and had a grand time. A few weeks after the campout, my son decided he wanted to cross over and join Patrick's troop. One night as we were preparing for the cross over, Patrick pulled me aside.

"I'm going to give you a year," he said cryptically. "A year for what?" I asked. "That's when you'll take over for me as Scout Master," he said calmly.

He and I hadn't worked together yet, and I didn't know what was involved in regard to time, attention, and effort. He didn't seem fazed by this at all. I asked him why he approached me. Weren't there other people who could step into this role?

"When we were on the campout, I watched how you interacted with the scouts and the parents. You were my choice. I saw you as my replacement. Remember, one year. You should tell your wife because I'm sure she sees what's coming too."

I lasted nine months. I didn't make it to the year allotment Patrick had given me. I became the Scoutmaster of Troop 941 and was grateful I did. I was in that role for five years, and twenty-seven young men became Eagle Scouts during that time. It is something that I will cherish for my lifetime. They did the work to earn every badge and rank. I was fortunate to get to know them and their families, and I saw them all grow into accomplished students and future leaders in their career.

As it got closer for my son to try and attain his Eagle Scout rank, I reached out to another father in the troop, Rich. His son had crossed over and I was now the observer. I pulled him aside one campout and said, "I'll give you a year . . ."

Rich stepped in after me just as I had stepped in after Patrick. This all started because Janet watched me at a meeting with a group of parents surrounded by a swarm of 6-year-olds. When my son was about to get his Eagle Scout rank, I ran into Janet in the local supermarket. It was great to see her again. After we caught up on all that our families had been doing, I asked her a question.

"Why did you ask me to lead all those years ago? I've loved the time that I've been involved, but I never knew why you asked."

"I saw you as a leader," she replied. "You see, many groups ask people if they'll volunteer or lead. Nine times out of ten they'll say 'No' because they're given the option to opt out. That isn't effective, and I needed people to take on roles. So I'd just gauge people's interest by watching them and then tell them that I saw leadership inside them. It has worked every time."

I was floored once again. This is an amazing approach that takes a mix of risk, faith, and a willingness to bet that being intentional will work out more often than not.

> **There's no reason you can't move the needle and start building leadership by opening doors.**

How would this look if you became an observer in your HR role? What would happen if you watched more instead of taking stock of people through some outdated system? Just think how leadership would look if you saw it in someone before you even gave them an opportunity. This approach runs contrary to almost every existing formulaic leadership model. The difference in this approach is that it works.

There's no reason you can't move the needle and start building leadership by opening doors. Once the door is open and a person walks in, you can develop them. If you reach their capacity, you can decide as an organization if that works for you. Chances are it will. The key is that you can lead as an observer of others. You need to have some checks and balances so that you aren't being biased either consciously or unconsciously. You can surround yourself with people who can be that fellow observers to provide consistency, diversity, and inclusion.

HR, I see this in you. It's time for you to see it in others.

CHAPTER 14

STAND IN THE GAP

WHEN IT COMES TO LEADERSHIP, people tend to think of those who are the most visible, vocal, and charismatic. That's natural because those actions are like a magnet for attention. We may not always concur with the ideas that are presented by these bright shining lights, but their allure is so strong that they are deemed "leaders." This mindset is like what you see in the world of celebrity. When someone exhibits some incredible talent or has a stunning physical appearance, crowds gather. Whatever traits are exhibited, people tend to put these performers on a higher platform than most people who see themselves as "regular."

It's unfortunate that humans tend to either sell themselves short of the talent they possess, or that they're so self-confident it borders on sheer arrogance. There seems to be very little middle ground. Please note that self-awareness is necessary for great leadership. Self-awareness does not mean being overly confident. In fact, many overconfident people are trying to cover and compensate for gaps that they don't want others to notice.

Can you lead and not be the loudest voice in the room?

Yes. Yes, you can. To make this happen though you need to shift how you approach the practice of human resources. Be forewarned that the next few suggestions run contrary to how leadership is noted and followed in most organizations. It is based far more on being observant than exerting a massive amount of energy and effort. It is subtle and even a bit manipulative. However, it works.

In the mid-1990s, companies in the US were caught up in the Quality Movement and great programs like ISO 9000 and ISO 9001 became important. People were seeking efficiency and standards which could be followed, measured, and implemented across various types of industries. At this time, I was the HR manager for a tool and die company. When I joined the company, they were swept up with many quality-oriented programs including the addition of self-directed work teams.

This was exciting to see because when the employees on the floor were broken into teams, the Operations VP asked other office-oriented staff to be the captain of these new teams. His fellow VPs were assigned teams as were the manufacturing engineers from operations. A problem arose when they didn't have enough white-collar staff to be captains of the blue-collar teams. I saw a chance to jump in, and even though I was relatively new to the company, I felt I could help facilitate a team. I experienced a typical response I have observed in organizations. The Ops VP gave me the most difficult employees that no one else wanted to work with. Now, he didn't tell me this. I found out later that he, and his two crony VPs, joked and laughed about how I was going to fail. Not cool to do to someone else, but you can't control the behavior of other "leaders."

This triumvirate was made up of the VPs of operations, finance, and sales—the three arms of this manufacturing entity. They were the most visible, vocal, and forceful three employees in the company. The owner felt confident that these three had the moxie to lead and drive the organization forward despite any other people working at the company. They often would have meetings just to shoot the breeze and complain about how others weren't nearly as effective as they were. It wasn't the healthiest environment at the top of the organization, but the other office staff and the front-line workers in the plant were wonderful humans. I related to them as my peers far more than I did in working with this leadership triangle of doom.

When the teams started to be formed, every other "captain" set up meetings on their calendars and called the men off the floor and away from production so that a proper meeting environment could be established. There were agendas, to-do lists, goals, and a list of tasks that were given based on each captain's observation of how their team was or wasn't performing. A schedule was created for subsequent meetings, and their self-directed teams plodded on. There was very little interaction from the machinists, and the captains would grouse about how they weren't making any significant headway.

When I was given the chance to meet my team, I did something completely different than what I had seen occur. I went out on the floor to the machinists at their stations. I was given the CNC lathe machinists. I got to work with Denny, Kyle, and Wallace. These three were artists. I mean it. They used CNC computers, which were the newest technology in the entire shop, and they would produce the most minute yet accurate pieces I had ever seen. When I came out to meet them, they all got skittish because they only thought HR came out to discipline folks. I explained that I was asked to be the captain of the CNC cell team. They howled with laughter!!

"What do you know about machining?" quipped Denny, the obvious leader of this crew.

"Nothing at all," I replied honestly.

"Then what are you doing out here?" Kyle snapped.

I pushed back without raising my voice or getting frustrated. I let them know that I felt I could get to know what they each did if I spent time with them each day talking to them and listening to them. I gave them the corporate line that everyone had to be on a self-directed work team, and I was here to stay. There were a few cuss words shared by the guys, and they shrugged and said, "Whatever."

I left them to return to their work, and the next afternoon I came back out on the floor and said, "So, how would you guys like to form this team?" They were astonished I had returned. They felt they had made it uncomfortable enough that I'd give up. "Well?" I asked. "How do you want to do this?"

Sarcastically Kyle said, "Let's come up with a team name."

"Perfect," I said. "Each of you come up with some ideas and when I come back out tomorrow, we'll pick a team name." As I was walking back to my office, I paused and looked back over my shoulder to see that the three of them were energized and scheming. I knew the next day would be interesting to say the least.

As promised, I came back out the following afternoon to ask if they had come up with any names. They had. They had a list of very crass and crude names that they shared amid peals of belly laughs. The laughs grew more raucous as they read each name because they became more and more vulgar. They looked at me, and I wasn't fazed.

"Interesting list. Which one do you like the best?" I asked. "I'm partial to _____." (I can't share what they were, but you need to trust me that they would make your hair curl.)

They couldn't believe that the HR manager wasn't losing his mind because of their childish prank. I honestly thought they were very creative in how they intertwined the words they had chosen. They thought I was going to either storm off in embarrassment or tell them how inappropriate they were. I didn't and pressed them to choose a name. They chose number two on the list and I wrote it as a header on the top of a piece of paper.

"Now that we have a name, how often would you like to meet?" I asked.

It was becoming obvious to the CNC crew that I was sticking to the task I was assigned. They thought I was okay since I passed their gauntlet of obscenities, and they started to warm up a bit. "What's the point of these teams?" Denny inquired.

I started to repeat the sentiments that were shared a week earlier at the all plant meeting when the self-directed teams were intro-duced. He stopped me and said, "I've heard this crap before. They (the management) aren't serious. They don't want us to improve. They just want us to keep cranking parts out. I don't buy this at all." Kyle and Wallace nodded in agreement. "We've seen pro-grams like this before," Wallace shared. "They come and go, and nothing changes."

I said, "That may be the case, but I'm new to the company and haven't been through these types of initiatives before. I'm willing to try if you are. Did you hear if our team comes up with something that saves costs you guys will get 10% of the savings? Wouldn't it be great if we tried to see if we could find something that made your work better and saved the company money too?"

They were skeptical but agreed to try. I told them that my role was just to facilitate and keep things moving. I'd offer support in any way I could including making connections with management and operations to try out their cost-saving ideas. We decided to check in every other day during the week so we could chat and monitor our progress. After a few weeks, the CNC three greeted me with smiles, laughter, and slaps on the back. I'd bring out coffee for each of them, and we'd catch up on their ideas as well as take time to talk about family, friends, and current events.

One day Denny pulled me aside and told me, "Steve, you know no one have ever given us attention and meant it. We usually get barked at by operations and engineering. No one is ever satisfied. It's different to have someone care and listen. Thanks for that."

I was touched and explained that meeting the team was a highlight of my day. I could hardly contain myself, wanting to come check in. I felt close to each of them and found that I admired their talent and contributions even more.

After two months, the team broke through. They came up with a method of holding the pieces that were being machined within tolerance. It would save the company . . . $100,000!! I was speechless this time. I asked if they were sure, and they showed me the pieces they had created to be the new holders, the math that affirmed their design, and the pieces they ran using their new system. I was geeked that they had come up with this amazing improvement.

I called for a meeting with the three VPs and my CNC team. This time we did meet in a conference room, and my team presented their invention and their findings. They also laid out the calculations of how their new system would save the projected $100,000 over a year's time based on the current level of pieces being produced. The VPs were impressed, and they told the team that they would implement their new system.

This is where you're supposed to cue the "happy ending" music as the camera fades out and you see text appear which shows the future steps of the three CNC men and their captain.

That didn't happen.

The VPs did implement the new system, but they took credit for the idea because they had "led" me in directing the team of machinists. They concocted some bogus story stating that it was inevitable that the operations and engineering team would have arrived at some system like this soon, and that my team was just lucky to figure it out. The owner of the firm listened to his tight circle of VPs and congratulated them on making this jump in quality.

My team never received any money for the savings they had projected and that had actually occurred. Not a dime. Denny and Kyle quit over the next six months and went to a competitor. The whole self-directed work team effort was scrapped because the HR guy had made it work and the traditional domineering captains had failed. The reason that was given to the plant employees was that this "team thing" took too much time and money. Neither reason was factual. I left that company as well because there was no way I was going to outlast the trio of VPs.

Even though the ending of this story didn't turn out as I had hoped, it did give me an experience that exhibited leadership that was far more impactful and potentially sustainable. Standing in the gap for the CNC crew was a more approachable, empathetic, and tangible form of leadership. I served as the facilitator and a partner in the process of seeing my team gel, develop, create, and succeed. They hadn't had someone from the office join them before and take an interest in their work and who they were as people.

Standing in the gap works. If you put yourself in a position where you are observant of the work going on around you, then you have the chance to pull different components together and move things forward. As an HR practitioner, you're surrounded by people from every department in your organization. You can look for ways that people and processes are disjointed or fragmented. These are opportunities to step in and lead.

Where are there gaps in processes happening today you could identify and intentionally step in? The work you could do would be so meaningful for you personally, and it could be the one component that has been missing to date. You don't have to be an expert in the field where the problem exists because by standing in the gap you build connections between people. When people are brought together, work has the ability to freely flow.

I was discouraged by the response from "leadership" after I had stepped in for my team. Through that disappointment I learned that my efforts were far more effective than the traditional approaches had been. I continue to a person who stands in the gap, and I encourage you do this as well. Someone has to stand up and show that all employees matter. It's a gap that needs to be filled.

CHAPTER 15

GRACE

HAVE YOU EVER made a mistake at work? Have you ever talked poorly about someone else you work with, or that you know, without that person knowing about it? Have you ever disappointed someone else because you didn't follow through on what you said you'd do? Have you ever said something that you thought was harmless, but it hurt someone deeply?

The answer for me is a resounding "Yes" to all the questions listed above. I'm not proud of that, but it's a reality. I'm human. I'm sure to fall and fail others. Hopefully it's not intentional, but it could be. I can fill this entire book with more questions that show how people fall short of positive or ideal behavior.

> The challenge in today's workplace, and in society overall, is that when we fail each other there is no room for grace.

The challenge in today's workplace, and in society overall, is that when we fail each other there is no room for grace. We demand an instant response along with a staunch stance to be taken with little room for any other position. We usually want others to hear our opinion, and we make arguments for others to come to our side. During this type of reaction, we completely run over our humanity.

Now, please understand that I'm talking about when someone makes a mistake and is insensitive or thoughtless about others and their feelings or diverse viewpoint. I'm not talking about overt actions and misconduct. That is a much deeper, and more concerning, level, and poor behavior should always be addressed. Even then though, I would offer that you should allow grace when entering these difficult situations.

As HR professionals, we are surrounded by people daily. (At least I hope you are!!) People are messy and will fail each other. It's unavoidable. When it occurs, we have a choice to either rely on a system of unrealistic policies and procedures as a list of do's and don'ts, or we can be humans ourselves.

We struggle with this because of the continued need for "account-ability." This is one of the most misinterpreted terms in organizations. Accountability should be defined as following through on what you commit to doing. However, more often than not, we misconstrue this term by alluding to the fact that accountability equals punishment. When it comes to situations involving employees, we often forget to breathe first. We jump to the nearest set of policies and comb through them to see what level of discipline needs to be metered out. It amazes me as an HR person that when employees slip up, the reaction is usually swift, harsh, and doesn't really take anything else into consideration.

Our systems of progressive discipline and layers of breaking Rule 1.0.1, Subsection A, litter our field with little regard of how these actions affect the person who broke said rule. We act as if they are the most disloyal, uncaring, and detrimental person who *ever* worked for the company.

Here's a question for you . . . Have you ever made a mistake or broken a rule at work?

Did the appropriate action take place? Were you written up, counseled, suspended, or fired? What if you were in this situation? How should the company treat you?

When I began working in the restaurant industry, I was disappointed by many of my HR peers. Instead of being geeked that I had found a new role, they piled on concern after concern that I wouldn't enjoy this new environment because restaurant employees and cultures made it difficult to do good HR. That was their opinion at least. Please note that few of these folks have ever worked in the restaurant industry, but that didn't stop them from sharing their opinions on the inevitable turnover present in hospitality jobs, the challenge of having a workforce that predominantly works part-time schedules on ever changing shifts, and the idea I'd be spending most of my time disciplining and terminating people. Astounding, simply astounding. Each facet of what they thought HR would be like in restaurants was either negative or daunting.

I didn't have any preconceived notions about working in restaurants. I looked at my new HR gig as a chance to work with a whole new batch of humans. When I took on this role, HR didn't have a good reputation internally either in the office or in our pizzerias. This was primarily because of the approach of my predecessor. They did a great job of establishing HR systems that hadn't existed in the past, but the company needed structure on the people side of the business. The difference that I brought to the mix was that I didn't believe HR needed to be practiced in a traditional manner that focused more on compliance than relationships.

Compliance needs to be respected because of the myriad of laws and regulations that cover and protect the workers, the workplace, and the company as a whole. Most situations and issues involving compliance are common sense. Also, you can be far more compliant when you have relationships with people because you can talk about the situation and the behavior they're exhibiting. Then you can give folks context around rules and systems. This is far more effective than ensuring people "stay in line."

Before I joined the company, HR typically showed up in the pizzeria when something needed to be "addressed." We rarely went out to visit just to see how people were doing. There had to be some sort of agenda item and purpose. The entire approach was task-oriented and transactional. Any visit was short, concise, and involved the least amount of conversation and personal interactions possible. This led the team members in the pizzerias to be apprehensive any time a person from HR appeared. Sound familiar?

I am not wired that way. I am probably far more conversational and relationship-focused than the average human. This is how I'm naturally wired. After my first few months being tied to my office and desk, I decided to venture out and visit our locations. Every time I entered a restaurant, I would get distrustful looks combined with a murmur of mumbling wondering why HR had come to visit. Who was in trouble? Who was getting fired? This barrier presented itself right as I hit the door, but I didn't get discouraged. In fact, it fueled my desire even more to break through the wall of negativity about HR.

There was one visit that helped me recalibrate team member interactions that I will always remember.

I was walking through the kitchen of one of our high-volume pizzerias when I saw a piece of paper mounted on one of the prep tables. It was at eye level, and you could tell it had been posted there to make sure the message was visible to every single employee. I had seen notes posted before, and I didn't care for them because they were usually a negative message. I felt that it showed that managers weren't talking to their staff. They were just dictating something that wasn't being performed or attended to. This note, however, was something I had never encountered before. It read:

"Look you motherf*#%ers, You need to put your f*#%ing glasses in the dishwashing area. If you bastards don't start doing this, you will be f*#%ing fired. The Management."

To say I was stunned would be an understatement. At first, I wasn't sure how to respond to what I just read. The first thing I did was look around at the other team members moving back and forth in the kitchen. No one seemed to be shocked, offended, or surprised by this mandate laced with creative language. It was fascinating!!

Before I tell you how I did respond, let me take a break to share how I assume many HR pros would have reacted . . .

The first response would be feigned offense, indignation, and disbelief. How could *anyone* allow this to be posted in the work environment? What were the managers thinking? The next step would be to tear the posting down in disgust with a tinge of embarrassment. Then, it was time to find out who was responsible for this obvious policy violation and hold them "accountable." This surely would result in some discipline. It could even mean a suspension with a good chiding, or even a termination. There wouldn't be joy in doing this, but the emotion of how awful this message from management was would have to be immediately dealt with and addressed. Heads would roll. An example would have to be made that this would never be tolerated *ever again*. Cue scary music in the background as the HR pro glares at the crumpled posting in their shaking hand.

Now let me share what really happened . . .

I carefully took the paper down and found the GM who happened to be working the shift. I calmly asked, "Having problems with team members and glasses?"

Their head dropped below their shoulders. "I didn't write that note. It was Louise." That didn't register with me because I didn't know who Louise was. "Is she a manager here?" I asked. "No, well, it's hard to describe," they stammered.

The GM went on to let me know that Louise was a long-term team member who came in very early in the morning to clean and get the store ready to be open every weekday. She had her own crew, but she wasn't officially a manager. She had been such a regular part of the store that she had seen managers come and go while she remained. I appreciated the background and asked if she was still at work. "Yes," they sheepishly replied. "She's right over there."

In the back of the kitchen stood an older, slender woman with an apron on. She was busily working, and the other team members seemed to enjoy being around her. I went up to her and introduced myself.

"Louise?" I asked, noticing I towered over her. I'm fairly tall, and she was not.

"Yep. Who are you? I've never seen you here before," she stated.

"I'm Steve," I replied.

"Uh huh. You from the office?" she wondered.

"Yes I am. I'm the new human resources director. Can I ask you about this note?" and I pulled out the instructions about how used glassware was to be properly placed.

"Oh yeah, I wrote that," she willingly admitted.

"Okay. Well, did you need to cuss when you wrote this? That's a pretty harsh way to describe our team members," I explained.

"Have you met some of them yet?" she calmly responded.

I laughed out loud. I know that may not have been the "proper" response from the HR 101 Operation Manual, but she caught me off guard, and it was funny.

"No ma'am. I haven't met many team members yet," I said.

She smiled back at me and said, "I suppose you don't want me to post my notes."

I wanted to make sure I had a good response for her. "I guess you're frustrated with others here. Would that be safe to say?"

"You're damn right I am. These kids don't have any work ethic. I come in here every f*#%ing day and pick up after them. Lazy f*#%ers. The whole bunch of them," she stated without batting an eye. It didn't matter that I was in human resources or from the corporate office.

She kept on going, but I stopped her and said, "Louise, I understand you're frustrated, but do you have to cuss when you're talking about others?"

"I don't f*#%ing cuss honey. I'm just talking." She meant it. She didn't even notice that she was swearing. Did I mention that Louise was in her early seventies during this encounter with me? I know that doesn't excuse coarse language, but it didn't really upset me. I had been around employees who swore during work for years. Many times, I joined in just so we could converse.

"Well Louise, I'm going to take down this note. I tell you what. I'll come visit you on a regular basis and you can share any frustrations you have with me, and we'll take a look at things. How does that sound?" I wasn't sure of the response I was going to get.

"I'd like that." She smiled again. "Nice to meet you."

I didn't write her up or discipline her. I crumpled up the sign and threw it out in a waste basket sitting next to us. I then left and went about my day, and so did she. The GM was watching our conversation the whole time. I'm sure they were curious to see how I was going to respond. We went to a part of the restaurant where we could talk, and she told me Louise's history. "She doesn't even know she's cussing, and the other team members love her. She loves them too. My restaurant is better with her in it. That's a fact."

I kept my commitment and visited Louise often. We grew very close, and she never stopped swearing. I learned about her family and how she had grown up with our founder's wife as a childhood friend. She was endearing just as the GM had told me.

I chose to respond with a tool that has worked for me my entire HR career when I found myself in these awkward circumstances. This is a very effective tool that is available for every person throughout your organization.

Grace.

This may be foreign to you, and I can almost guarantee that it's foreign to how employees have been approached in the past. We don't feel that we have the latitude in our roles to show grace to others when they mess up. I just don't think it's true. We can take ownership of how we approach others with our own personal style.

I know that when others have shown me grace when I've stumbled, I've been thankful. It allowed both of us to breathe, calm down, and look at the situation in a fresh and open way.

Often, it led to a productive outcome and a stronger relationship. Trust me when I say that allowing grace in our interactions with others will result in a positive experience most of the time.

I'm not saying that discipline and termination are never warranted at work. However, I use a yardstick that says that you only need to implement these steps based on an employee's behavior and actions. Even with that benchmark, I still review each case and consider all of the factors as well as the person who's about to be disciplined. I want them to come out of any conversation understanding the situation, its context and how we move forward from there.

Now, so you don't think I'm being utopian or an idealist, understand that I practice this both inside work and outside of work. It's not a popular position. Most people want a pound of flesh when they are wronged. I'll hold out until the last possible moment before making difficult decisions because I believe in people, even in the darkest situations.

You see, I make mistakes and I have disappointed others—even those closest to me. How can I expect grace from others if I am not willing to be graceful myself? Also, how will others show grace if it isn't given to them?

I recommend that you try a new approach and allow grace to occur.

I'd also recommend that you make grace the norm when people work with each other regardless of their position and level in your company. If you can teach those who manage people the power of this tool, you'll see a genuine shift in how people treat each other. It's time for us to buck the trend of others who tend to be reactive and destructive when people fail them. Instead of talking *about* others, talk *to* them with an attitude of grace first so that you seek to understand them, the situation they're facing, and the way to move forward. If you try this, you'll see people aren't as bad as you think. It will also make HR, and your life, more balanced and fulfilled. It works.

One last note . . .

I had worked with Louise for over a decade when age started to finally catch up with her. She had lasted through two additional GMs since we first met. They moved on to other stores in our chain and she remained a constant. She had to retire when her memory started to fade, and she's living in an assisted living facility now. The last GM to work with her had kept a folder with her notes that she had posted in it. When she was getting ready to leave on her last day, he showed Louise the folder and said, "This will always be here in the store because we want you to always be here with us."

That, my friends, is grace.

CHAPTER 16

WORK FROM THE CORE

HAVE YOU EVER TRIED to regularly exercise? I remember when I was a teenager, being active was natural. You didn't have to exercise per se. You may have been part of some athletic endeavor which required time in the gym on the weights or some extensive running regiment, but not everyone was in sports. As I age, I have started to exercise for general health because I find myself sitting far more than I do moving around. One of the realities of consciously being active again is various levels of soreness and aches. Ironically, trying to eliminate aches was what got me back into the gym.

Exercise can be done in many different ways, and no one way works for everyone. I tend to do a mix of walking, treadmills, ellipticals, and shooting basketball. I want to make sure that I'm not only doing one type of activity all the time. I hope that my entire body is involved over the course of gym visits throughout the week. The key is not to lull myself into a pattern where only certain parts of my body get the benefit from working out.

Organizations tend not to exercise. They fall into patterns where the same activity gets repeated over and over. If an area does see activity, it's on the fringes and away from the core of who they are and the products or services they produce. Whenever an extreme situation or circumstance appears, everyone turns their efforts towards thwarting this anomaly. The reaction is warranted, and it is better to operate from a place of balance and harmony. However, this "rush to the problem" method is exhausting. Everything can't be a call to arms.

Whenever companies keep their eyes out for the exception, a critical part of the enterprise starts to fail. The core of the business may continue to function, but it isn't doing so in the most optimal way. It can't because everyone is rushing here and there to keep working on the fringes. If the core of a business atrophies and begins to falter, then you run the risk of performance degrading everywhere.

We need to recognize that when a company's focus is primarily directed out on the borders, employees also become discouraged. All people want to have stability and a centralized base from which to do their work. It gives us a sense of reassurance and purpose. You can't overestimate the power of having work aligned with a person's daily expectations. This doesn't mean that there shouldn't be variety. There should be. One thing to note is that variety is vastly different than the daily fire alarm which may or may not be real.

HR needs to take heed of practicing on the fringes. Unfortunately, most policies and procedures in place within companies today were based on exceptions. A few examples of poor behavior occurs, and a new policy instantly is created. Working from the fringes in HR is especially detrimental for a company because that means the majority of employees are overlooked. At the same time, the new enforcements (a better word for policies) just add more and more confusion and restriction. The truth is that they aren't needed, but it's what we're used to doing.

I think we have a chance to turn things around by acknowledging something and completely altering our mindset. This isn't going to be easy because "work" as we know it has long been based on this mental attitude. If you're willing to try to move away from this approach, you can make a lasting difference and lead in a way that is overdue.

Here it is: Everything can't be broken.

This is the current justification of why anyone has a job. Sure, people need to work in order to earn a wage and provide for themselves and others in their lives, but if you ask people why they work, they tell you they're necessary because *everything* is a problem. They don't have a single aspect of their job that isn't broken or in disrepair.

This isn't true. It never has been. We have come to believe that we exist in our companies to solve problems. Without problems, there's no reason to come in. I know that's a broad generalization, but it seems to be the case when you talk to people about their day. They release a heavy sigh and bemoan the mountain of insurmountable obstacles they must tackle. Ironically, HR has concocted systems which perpetuate this mindset. We reward those who are problem solvers through both compensation and higher positions.

Problem solving is needed because problems do naturally arise in the course of daily business. However, it shouldn't be the primary effort of someone's day. I think this takes some reframing of how we look at work.

Instead of everything being broken, we could look at daily activity from a positive perspective. The expectation could be that we are going to perform. If "performance" is the foundational block we work from, then problems will fall into place and be addressed as we strive for even better performance. I understand that this is semantics, but words have such power and impact that something as simple as performance vs. problems can give employees encouragement and not dread.

> **HR can stand alongside others throughout the organization and be encouragers.**

When my kids were young, my wife and I encouraged them any time they hit a subject where they stalled. We patiently sat with them to help them to think through whatever they were stuck on. In return, we'd experience a range of emotions ranging from frustration to anger to tears. If we stayed the course and kept encouraging them, they'd eventually work their way to the desired result. Their efforts in working through what they faced allowed them to both learn and perform.

HR can stand alongside others throughout the organization and be encouragers. This behavior allows people to work from the core of their role. Instead of picking at what someone doesn't do, you can make the time to assess what's in front of people and coach them up and through. Letting people know that they can look at work from different angles and perspectives allows them to bring the positive aspects of creativity into their normal working process.

Organizations aren't broken. They're just performing at differing levels and paces. Let's do what we can to make performance our core.

Here's a new approach to consider. In his seminal TED talk, Simon Sinek talked about the "Golden Circle," a model that shows how most organizations work from the outside ring toward the middle. The three rings are: What (the outermost ring), How (the middle ring) and Why (the innermost ring). He contends that companies start with What and move to How. They rarely get to Why. He makes a compelling argument that when you turn your approach around and "start with why," you will be far more successful in your efforts in both the short and long term. I recommend that you check out his TED talk and even pick up the book he penned from this talk: *Start with Why*.

Using that same model construct, put your employees in the rings as follows:

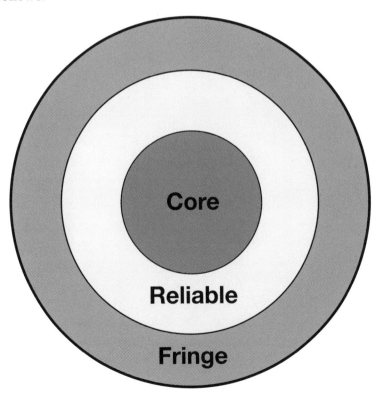

We gravitate toward the same behavior that Sinek describes. We start, and focus mainly, with those employees who are on the fringe regarding behavior. When we do this, we ignore the middle ring of reliable employees. This is unfortunate because the folks who make up the reliable ring are the fabric that keep the company functioning. They're thoughtful and do their best work each and every day. The people in the core have proven themselves to be more critical to the success of the company than even the reliable employees. These are the people whom the company views as assets they'd like to keep, develop, and grow for the present and the future.

If that's the case, then what would our company look like working from the core? If we started with the core and gave them our time and attention instead of assuming that they'll always be with us, think of the shift that would occur. You can work with core employees to reach out, focus on, and develop the employees in the reliable ring. Then you can address the fringe employees only when it's necessary. Trust me. If you're able to make this model come to life in your organization, the fringe employees will leave. It may be because of their behavior, or because they just don't feel they're getting the attention they're trying to garner.

With this model, you can encourage and show the fringe employees the path to become a reliable employee. Likewise, you can develop reliable employees to become part of the core. If you can picture two arrows in the model of how to work with employees, you'll see movement that provides a healthier, and possibly more inclusive, culture for everyone.

The first arrow begins in the Core and points out to the Fringe. This represents how to prioritize your time and daily interactions with employees. The core employees should get more of your time and attention at all organizational levels and through every department. The second arrow travels from the Fringe to the Core and shows the path where you create and implement your training and development activity. Give people the opportunity to move away from the Fringe and toward the Core by intentionally coaching and equipping them.

These arrows allow employees to find their place. This model also gives HR and senior leadership a road map from which you can have performance discussions, identify future leadership, and build a general format around people. With this tool, you can establish a common language based on those who work for you now and in the future.

Combine the expectation of performance with the framework for employees to live and function inside of, and you land on the ability to work from the core.

CHAPTER 17

DON'T BE A BOBBLEHEAD

EVERYONE HAS THEIR QUIRKS. Most of the time we keep them to ourselves, but I'm cool with you knowing one of mine. I'm a collector. Not a hoarder, a collector. I have always collected things that interest me. When I was young, I was even trying to reach a world record collecting bottle caps from soda bottles with my younger brother. We ended up with over 20,000 bottle caps that we stored in an old console TV box in our garage. Our mom was not a fan, but she let us continue our adventure to see if we'd reach our goal. We never contacted the folks at the *Guinness Book of World Records*, but we loved gathering all of the bottle caps.

Since my childhood, I've curbed my collections (somewhat). Now I only have collections of marbles, fossils and rocks and . . . bobbleheads. I think they're fun. Little statues of various figures whose heads toss to and fro whenever you jostle them. Now I know there are bobbleheads for all sorts of things these days like TV shows, movies, and even cartoon characters. I am more of a "purist" and collect bobbleheads from my favorite sports teams. They capture a point in time and show players that were popular or legends from the organization's history. Living just outside the city of Cincinnati, I am a Cincinnati Reds fan. They are an iconic professional baseball team, the very first professional team to be established back in the late 1800s. I try to attend several games a year, and I make a special effort to go if they're going to hand out bobbleheads of the players.

> **HR folks are great implementers when we could be great instigators!!**

I'm very cool with collecting bobbleheads but not with being one. Unfortunately, I feel that many HR pros act like bobbleheads within their organizations. Often we find ourselves nodding in acceptance of senior management because we don't want to rock the boat. We may not agree with what is being said, but we don't push back. We just do our best to make things happen. There is value in being a peacemaker in an organization but not in being passive. HR has wrongly believed that if we "keep the peace," we're being effective.

HR folks are great implementers when we could be great instigators!!

Acceptance for acceptance's sake diminishes our role in organizations. Great leaders in senior management don't want people who just say "Yes" and bobble their head up and down. They expect people to give their input and have meaningful discussions as well as offer potential solutions. When HR continues the myth of waiting for some special invitation from senior managers to engage and be strategic, we are fooling ourselves. Leadership is an expectation based on participation and action. It isn't something bestowed upon people.

Our aversion to taking risks keeps HR on the outside looking in. It's understandable that we are tasked with being risk mitigators, but it shouldn't force us into a position that keeps us outside the mix of the regular movement of the business. I would contend that staying idle and always taking the mild and undistinguished stance hurts us personally and professionally. HR shouldn't be the doormat of acceptance in an organization.

I'm not suggesting you should become argumentative and disagreeable. It's intriguing to me that when people are given advice on a possible direction to take, we tend to become a pendulum that swings too far. If we've been silently agreeable in order to keep things in harmony and balanced, it seems foreign to now be a outspoken champion of all things people-related. You don't have to become something so opposite of what may have been your approach. If you do make a pendulum swing, you will feel awkward and uncomfortable. It will be just as ineffective and being the constant affirmation source.

I want to encourage you to consider taking on a new posture as an HR pro. Historically, HR has been stereotyped in one of two ways when we respond to employee situations. We're either tagged as the people who always say "No" because we're viewed as restrictive rule mongers, or we say "Yes" to keep balance and harmony. I think there's a better response.

"It depends . . ."

On the face of it, this response seems extremely non-committal and guarded. When I've given people from other departments an "It depends" response, they hate it. The only reason people hate that response is because they want an instant "Yes" or "No" answer, so you agree and support their perspective and position on what they're presenting. Now, if you say "It depends" only to buy time and hope things get better, that's poor as well. Using this phrase allows you to look at all sides of a situation. The key is to follow that response with a decisive stance base on your expertise.

We are fortunate as HR practitioners in that we get to work with every human in the company. I understand that some of this interaction may be indirect, but you are more connected to employees than other departments. You can be a leader by helping people assess the situations they face. There are very few instances where an immediate answer is needed. Using "It depends" sets the stage for assessment with the understanding that you will land on an answer. We can't lose sight that our decisions regarding people can affect them as a person. It would be better for all HR pros and organizations if we sought a positive outcome instead of looking for curtness and expediency as our motivator.

When you offer an analysis and assessment of employee interactions, you're allowing various options and angles to be considered. In the end, you'll come to a conclusion that will have a longer lasting positive result. This positioning gives us a stronger stance from which to lead. HR has the obligation to lead in organizations and not settle for being a support function that nods its head.

The bobbleheads I collect are kept on a bookshelf. They're cool to look at, but without movement they spend most of their time collecting dust. We don't have to be bobbleheads. We can be a critical and sought-after resource in our companies. Choose to be involved. You'll see that working with people will be far more rewarding when you are involved with others and not just offering a simple "Yes" or "No."

CHAPTER 18

CRUSHING INERTIA

HAVE YOU EVER had the blahs at work? Every day seems to be monotonous and repetitive. You yearn for variety but can't see how it can happen. We don't want to ever admit this because we're afraid if we express this feeling of malaise to others, we'll lose our job. This is difficult because every person throughout an organization hits these lulls. It doesn't matter if you're a front-line employee or a CEO.

How about you as an HR practitioner? Have you ever felt stuck and mired in your circumstances? I'm sure you have. It is more common than we think. Please note that being stuck isn't a matter of disengagement. You can be stuck and have passion, energy, and drive. However, you still may not be able to escape that sinking feeling.

You may have never thought that organizational behavior is tied to physics, but it is. Whenever people find themselves in a rut, we're battling inertia. Inertia is "a tendency to do nothing or to remain unchanged" according to the *Oxford English Dictionary*. If you've ever studied physics, you understand that inertia is an incredibly difficult thing to break. Once things settle in, they're more likely to seek being comfortable than wanting to shift. So it's not surprising that employees hit stretches where they're floating and going through the motions.

There are some indicators when inertia is starting to take hold. The first is ironically a flurry of busyness. When you go through your workspace at the beginning of the day, ask how people are doing. They will tend to tell you they are "fine" to be polite, and then when you press about their workload, they'll tell you they're "busy." They are. People, for the most part, are hard workers who are both conscientious and have a desire to do their best. We need to face that activity does not automatically equate to productivity. Activity does equate to being busy. It's important to note the employees who are great producers will let you know they are full but they're not feeling "busy."

Another indicator of inertia is deflection. When you ask a person for a status update on a project, you get an indirect response. You hear a mix of excuses, failures of others to keep their commitments, and a denial of accountability. A good deflector can get you to turn your attention away from them and focus on something completely unrelated. If you shift to follow these distractions, you allow people to remain in place, which is their real desire. We've all deflected. There may be times when you need more time to complete the work you are tasked with, but it should be the exception and not a regular practice.

Deflectors can be far more destructive than those who are busy. The reason for this is that a person adept at the smoke and mirrors approach can advance and get promoted. I'm sure you know of people who've moved into senior roles and you're not quite sure what they've ever accomplished. This isn't a good thing for organizations. There needs to be more attention on what a person is and isn't contributing through regular observation. You can't only rely on performance management systems conducted to varying degrees of regularity and success.

A third indicator of inertia is a shift in behavior and disconnectedness. Mental health is a driving factor of every employee. Every employee who comes to work is experiencing life in some form or fashion. People don't have the same life experiences, and we often overlook this. At times, we try to suppress life's ups and downs and believe they shouldn't be part of the workplace. You have employees who come from constructive, supportive home environments working alongside those who have a much different home life. This variety cannot, and should not, be contained or constricted. When we try to squeeze the life out of people, we see a feeling of discouragement instead of support. Over time, this slows people down until they get stuck.

We can't afford to be stuck personally. Whenever we lapse into autopilot, we aren't doing what we were called to do: move the organization forward. It's critical that we are aware of how inertia is affecting us and others. By doing this, you can assist in helping others break free from the grip of mediocrity. It takes a considerable amount of effort and attention, and each's person's degree of "stuckness" varies. Some may be just going through a season whereas others may be so mired that drastic action may need to happen. Just as in all circumstances working with people, no situation is the same as the next. We need to break from the "one size fits all" approach to human resources that has never worked in practice. Ever.

Since people are individuals, you will find that you are far more effective practicing HR from a basis of focusing on each person for themselves. This will feel unsettling because we are more comfortable throwing out a blanket solution or program to try and cover all people regardless of what they're personally facing. Being stuck is a personal obstacle. Unattended it can become a collective obstacle that affects groups, departments, or even entire business units. It's nearly impossible to go after a large chunk of inertia. You don't possess the energy or stamina to make much of a dent. However, when you work with people one-on-one, you can get people moving more easily. Over time, as you get more individuals unstuck, the collective eventually moves as well.

How do you get people moving? What steps can you take to get them out of their funk? As mentioned before, it depends. I have found one surefire cure that you can implement, but it involves an action that not everyone is adept at.

People are not meant to be isolated and alone. We were wired from the dawn of time to seek connection with other people. When people experience isolation, they are more assuredly going to get stuck. They don't have anyone around them to impact their daily activity or behavior. More often now than ever before, an employee can be working amid a large number of people and still be, or feel, alone. Loneliness occurs in all sizes of companies and throughout all industries. Just because you physically see bodies milling around the workspace in offices, cubicle farms, manufacturing floors, or worksites in the field doesn't mean that anyone present in those environments is truly connected with each other. We assume that because people are talking with each other during the normal course of business, then they must be connected. This is a bad assumption.

HR has the opportunity to make sure that people are both anchored and tethered to others. We can make introductions and be intentional in checking in on our employees, regardless of their level or title, and see if they have one or two anchors. Anchors are people who act as a sounding board, an idea creator, or an empathetic audience for someone else. When you have one or two anchors at work, you feel grounded. You can go to them and they can come to you. These relationships are mutual and reciprocated. Having anchors gives you a sense of reassurance and, hopefully, encouragement. This allows a needed outlet because you can release anxiety, concern, anger, joy, etc. Anchors are an emotional component that can help people recharge and move forward. They are key to breaking inertia.

Being tethered helps people build a web of connections that give them various paths to move and maneuver easily in their work. When we have paths of people to go to as needed, we are less likely to remain isolated. By establishing these webs and making sure that humans are tethered to each other, then you can observe work as it goes through its natural ebbs and flows. Also, when the strands of the web break, it's easier to spot and address. Tethered strands can break for a variety of reasons ranging from personal work styles to unforeseen life circumstances that pop up. You see webs alter and take on new shapes when people are promoted and they become "in charge" of a set of people. Webs also shift when a member leaves your circle of employees internally within the company or they leave the company altogether.

Anchored and tethered people will start doing what people do. They will form relationships that have good seasons and dry seasons. There will be push, pull, conflict, and accomplishments that present themselves at different times and at different levels of intensity. While this happens, the key is that people continue to generate ongoing efforts and energy, which means there is movement. Movement is needed to thwart inertia. We need to do our best to always keep moving even if it's at a snail's pace. You will experience bursts of sprinting at times, but hopefully those will be exceptions because, like it or not, our race never ceases at work.

What is important to remember is that when you step in through your HR role to cultivate and shepherd people, you're providing the fuel to combat the most subtle enemy of productivity. So, to make sure you don't just identify anchors and tethers for others, you need to be intentional yourself in making sure you have anchors and tethers too. This may be difficult within the structure of your organization because our jobs and responsibilities can unfortunately isolate us. Once we recruit, hire, and on-board people, we release them to their work group. We may get to touch base with them every so often, but they're now needed in other places. Then, we are most likely the last person someone encounters when they leave the company either on their own or as a result of a failure in behavior. It presents a challenge for us to have anchors internally because we work with, and know all of, the "stuff" of employees.

I'd encourage you to find an anchor or two externally. Just as we were never intended to be alone in life as people, HR was never meant to be practiced as an island. Find a peer who can be your anchor and be an anchor for them. For you to be the great HR leader you want to be, you need to be grounded and healthy yourself. Make the effort to reach out and get an anchor. You'll find that this will make you more potent and will keep you unstuck as well.

Inertia is a beast waiting to crush you and others. Fight the urge to become complacent by having those few essential connections in your personal and professional life. Then, put on your work clothes to jump in and keep others moving. It will be some of the most rewarding work you will ever experience!!

CHAPTER 19

BE A LIGHTHOUSE

I HAVE A THING FOR LIGHTHOUSES. They are incredibly intriguing structures. Whenever my family goes on vacation, they know that if we are near a lighthouse, I'll make it a stop to check out. Over the years, I've visited and climbed up into several lighthouses. Even though each of them is a vertical tube that shoots into the sky, not one of them is the same. I can't get enough of them. My wife has resigned herself to the fact that I will go out of my way to find lighthouses. I'm even trying to convince her to go on a trip where we'd travel up the coastline to stop and see each lighthouse that dot the beaches and cliffs. This is a bucket list item for me.

Other than their unique appearance and placement, I am fascinated by lighthouses because of their purpose and function. Unfortunately, most lighthouses these days are tourist attractions and few of them are in service. When they were active, they provided assistance to countless ships and vessels. What seems to be a simple set of actions honestly saved the lives of hundreds or thousands of those who worked at sea. Each lighthouse had a keeper who was responsible for its maintenance and performance. They lived either at the base of the lighthouse or in a structure nearby so they could make sure the beacon that emanated nightly was ready to go.

The life of a lighthouse keeper was often bleak and full of uncertainty. The lenses at the top of their tower needed to be polished and cleaned so the beam of light would be as bright as possible. It couldn't be blurry or dull because that may mean that a ship would hit something unknown just below the water's surface, or worse yet, the coastline itself. A keeper may have a family that lived with them, but they would experience the same lifestyle of the keeper. Almost all of their time was focused on the lighthouse. Sailors relied on the lighthouse to be consistent and visible. The blazing shaft of light that shot out to pierce the darkness was the result of endless attention and a multitude of steps that needed to be followed every time the light came to life.

Whenever I've spent time visiting lighthouses, I make sure to meander around the keeper's living quarters to try and imagine what life was like for them. Then, after I've climbed up to the top of the lighthouse, I imagine once again the rotation of the lens and the brilliant beacon that would stand out in the pitch black. It gets me all geeked each time I experience it. It never gets old.

I compare human resources to both the lighthouse and the keeper. There are many similarities that should lift you up instead of seeing what we all do with dread.

I believe that HR is critical for organizations. Whenever you have two or more people who work together, HR exists. We are in the business of helping employees live and work in a way whereby everyone contributes and is valued. This may seem like a lofty justification for human resources as a profession, but it's more than that. Human resources exists whether there is someone who fills a position or not. We can't keep thinking of HR as only a job description. If your company understands that they can bene-fit from having a keeper or two, then I think they have a better chance of people navigating safely through the seas of work.

HR is a lighthouse because we can be the beacon that cuts through the darkness that presents itself far too often. I'm not talking about being the Happy Committee that pumps out listless messages that everything is rosy all of the time. Since people are that combination of being messy *and* wonderful, some-one needs to bring light to the daily congregation of the workplace. If there isn't some-one providing light, dark-ness is sure to envelop the

> **Being positive should serve as an unbreakable foundation for our profession.**

surroundings, and shipwrecks will be littered all throughout the company. Being positive should serve as an unbreakable founda-tion for our profession. This has to be as sturdy as the towers of light that are build straight up from the ground.

This may not be a popular sentiment, but I feel that those in HR who don't project light in the darkness should consider going into another career. It's time we see how the impact of bringing a positive perspective into the workplace can make a culture truly become a workplace that entices and retains people. Our actions are far more lasting than scoring well on some internal employee satisfaction survey. Instead of following the practices of other HR functions that issue survey after survey, we should be out among our people as light. This will give people confidence that they are seen, acknowledged, and valued. These three components are far more essential to actual engagement than any survey response.

Lighthouses also show the way to safety when rough seas are present. There is always turmoil, conflict and differences of opinion at work. When people work together, these storms can happen. Since we know that waves are going to rise and crash against people to get them off course, someone needs to break through to help them steer through conflict. In organizations, we tend to complain outside of conflict when we could respectfully work through it. Imagine what your workplace would be like if complaining lessened, people addressed each other, and we removed the ability for people to be passive aggressive. It would be magnificent!! Moving through conflict needs a lighthouse just as much as avoiding the angry waves all together.

We have the chance to be great lighthouse keepers. Yes, at times this means that we're on the outside looking in because our work is ideally from an objective viewpoint. We need to be looking out over the sea and coastline that we are responsible for. We should be diligent in watching all of the many ships coming into port as well as those going back out to sea, bobbing up and down with the waves. This movement is constant and ever-changing. It takes someone who understands that being a keeper is critical. They serve as the role that ensures safe passage to and fro. You can lead as a keeper from the lighthouse, clearing up unseen barriers so the other ships can do their jobs.

There are tasks you may have to perform that you will see as mundane and insignificant. They may not get as much attention as other functions in the company because they are behind the scenes. You may meet with two people and "fix" their relationship without any kudos or acknowledgment. That's okay. It's more important for others to follow the beacon from the lighthouse than the keeper. When a keeper is credible, accessible, and available to perform their duties, the lighthouse does its job. Take heart and know that when you're a keeper, your work shines everywhere. It becomes what people come to expect, knowing that when you're in place, they're able to do their work. Every company needs a lighthouse . . . and a keeper.

CHAPTER 20

BRIDGE BUILDING

WE ALL ARE CAUGHT UP in our day-to-day roles. There's value in that because having some assurance that work is waiting you when you head into work each day is grounding. Whenever you ask people if they'd rather be full of work or empty wondering when the next task will arrive, they'll choose full every time. This is true even if they aren't all keyed up about the work they do. We strive to be full, or even overloaded, most of the time. We tell ourselves that if we're busy, then we're needed.

Most people connect their personal identity and worth with their occupation. We can have aspirations of a balance between work and "life," but they are so intertwined that the truth is that each area gets a certain amount of time and focus simultaneously. There may be clean breaks where you're only doing work commitments or enjoying life experiences in separate time frames. When that happens, make sure to relish both areas. Think of how our jobs would look like if we were able to have clean separation of the areas of our lives easily. Ah, to dream!!

Because we're filled to the brim with activity, it's difficult to pull back and reflect, plan, and strategize. We constantly feel pulled back into the rushing waters where we spend most of our time. The sentiment is that we just can't afford to step away. We've bought into the mental myth that if we dare step away from our normal routine, our world will collapse. That may happen to a few people, but I think it's the exception far more than the rule.

In my current role, we have adopted a practice that is contrary to other companies I've worked for. When you're out of the office for vacation or to attend a conference, you're not expected to call in. Seriously. We believe that you should be paying attention to what's in front of you and not what's potentially happening back at the office. I remember that the first vacation I took after joining this company, I called my boss to check in on Monday. I'll never forget this conversation and his admonition.

"Steve, how's your vacation so far? Why are you calling in?" my boss asked gently.

"Well, um, I was just, um, checking in to make sure everything was okay and if anyone needed anything from me," I responded, a bit confused.

"We're fine. Nothing's going on. I need you to remember something, Steve," he said.

"What's that?"

"We've been in business for fifty years successfully without you. Now, go and enjoy your family and your vacation," he said positively.

There was silence on my end of the call. I tried to respond and explain why I felt compelled to call in, but he had already hung up. Since that first vacation, I've taken the time to break away and recharge, which is the intention of any time off from our regular job. He wasn't being harsh. He was just trying to reframe my perspective and turn me towards a much healthier direction.

We need to have time to step out of the normal course of business. If we are running all of the time, we will be more prone to mistakes and possibly suffer burnout over time. It's key to remember that even though we add value to the company, it can exist without us. We're not that important. That may be hard to hear, but my boss's comment is the truth.

Since that's the case, how can we make sure that the time we contribute to our role and our company has merit? I think we need to model the example that was shared with me after a conference where I spoke.

I had just come off the stage after giving a presentation at an HR conference when someone who was kind enough to attend approached me. You need to know that after an hour-long presentation, I am spent. I'm a high energy person who tries to lay all of my intensity out completely any time I get to lead a session. I was trying to grab something to drink and replenish myself when this very exuberant person grabbed my attention.

"Steve, do you have a second?" he asked excitedly.

"Sure," I said a bit reluctantly.

Undaunted, he jumped straight in. "Great!! Loved your presentation. Got some fantastic takeaways that I'm going to try to implement when I get back to work. I just wanted to tell you about my new HR role. I thought you'd relate to it." His energy reinvigorated me the more he spoke. You could feel his joy and desire to share what he was experiencing.

"My new boss recently pulled me aside like yours did in your story and he asked me, 'Do you know why you're here at this company?' Sound like when your boss asked you in the past?" He made sure I agreed before continuing.

"My boss told me that I was hired as their first HR manager for two reasons. The first was to make sure to take care of 'his people'—the employees. The second reason he explained was that I was tasked to make sure that his legacy remained after he left the company. He didn't want all that he and his other founding employees had built to disappear. He asked me if I liked the culture so far, and I told him that it was the best one I had known over my career. Then he said again, 'That's my legacy. You need to be the bridge to make sure that our great culture survives.' Isn't that awesome?!"

I told him it was awesome and thanked him for taking time to tell me his story. He was fortunate enough to have found an HR role that had organizational meaning along with personal purpose for him. That should be the ideal for anyone practicing HR. After hearing his story, it made me wonder. What could we do as HR professionals to put us in a similar position as he now found himself? Then, it hit me. His new boss said it.

Be the bridge.

Bridges are a common part of our lives. They're probably too common because few bridges gain our attention. There are exceptions of some magnificent structures here and there throughout the world. Most bridges, however, are functional structures that connect two areas together. Bridges blend in even though they serve an incredible purpose. What would happen on your regular commute to work if every bridge you crossed wasn't present? It would cause a massive traffic jam that would dwarf the already messy congestion many people face.

HR is essential in organizations. I've heard arguments for eliminating the human resources function often. When you hear descriptive phrases like "necessary evil," it can be discouraging. Whenever a company gets to a point that HR is either unnecessary or an "evil," it's because we've earned it by being distant, isolated, or utilized only in dire emergencies. I have heard from many HR pros who struggle with being put in these boxes, and they aren't sure how to get out. They grumble and succumb to this detrimental classification of their roles and contributions.

Being a bridge builder will eliminate this jaundiced view of who we are and what we do. You can lead by being a connector. In fact, it may be some of the most powerful leadership that can transpire in an organization. The challenge in taking steps to build bridges is that you must have the fortitude to take the first step. This step may seem easy on the surface, but many people struggle to make it happen.

Lift your head up out of the weeds.

It's impossible to build bridges without assessing the landscape and environment around you. If you are keeping your head down because you're so "buried" with work, you'll never recognize where bridges could bring folks together. Someone has to lift their head up because nearly everyone else at your workplace has their head down also. The only times you see people's faces are when they enter their work space or when they get up to stretch, take a bio break, or grab something to eat. Once they've accomplished their break, their face turns down once again either to a screen or a hands-on task that requires their attention.

I'm sure you've noticed silos which exist all around you. Organizations are still built in hierarchical pyramids which get extremely narrow at the top. The org chart shows lines of reporting relationships and levels of assumed authority, but those aren't bridges. Remember, you can travel both ways on bridges.

Hierarchies aspire to promote two-way communication and inter-action and may even have rallies, training, or the occasional moti-vational poster hung to support those aspirations. The actuality is that most actions in companies flow one way . . . down.

Bridges are needed everywhere. You can build short ones that connect two people together, so they are more effective in their work. You can take the next step and build bridges between departments or business units. These bridges take a little more effort, infrastructure, and attention, but connecting silos is the best way to destroy them. We need to stop complaining that silos exist (including HR), and do something to constructively elimi-nate them. Bridging silos together does that. If you're someone who is a bridge builder to ensure productive, healthy working relationships and also construct some bigger departmental structures, you're being a successful leader. Companies would flourish by having these types of bridges connecting across func-tions in order to have an environment and culture that exhibits its connectedness.

You could also be adventurous and take on building bridges across an entire organization. This may mean that you need to be in a senior leadership role, but not necessarily. It takes some-one with vision, determination, and a willingness to take risks to put together an organization-wide bridge. Remember, there are few bridges that are instantly recognizable throughout the world. Bridges like the Golden Gate Bridge in San Francisco, California, the Tower Bridge in London, England, and the Harbour Bridge in Sydney, Australia, are works of art that happen to also serve as ribbons of transportation and commerce. Putting together the pieces that span an entire organization are works of art as well. Why can't HR be the one to create these masterpieces?

Remember, we're in the people business, and organizations are crawling with people. Building a large-scale bridge requires you to be strategic so that you foresee any potential places where the bridge could fail. Doing this work isn't a series of tasks. It's a series of calculated guesses to build something that will cover a true chasm. It has to be able to bend, flex, and contort in order to stay upright and functioning in the ever-moving flow of work.

This may be a reach for you, but I would encourage you to not only lift your head up, but also stretch a bit to see out over the horizon of where your company exists. An organizational connector may be needed. You may be the architect that sees it and brings along a team of others to make your vision a reality.

Bridges do one more thing which my friend shared. They establish a legacy and an identity. Whenever a company can show cohesiveness across its functions, it becomes a true employer of choice. No survey is needed to confirm that because the people who work there live it. Think of how satisfying your role in HR would be on a regular basis if you approached it as someone who was forging a company's legacy and identity. It makes me shiver with excitement and anticipation.

My friend is experiencing this, and honestly, so am I. I've been fortunate to work in roles and organizations that needed bridges built, and I've relished the chance to put them up. This is an opportunity that is within your grasp. It's time to scan your company to see where bridges are needed, and then get out your blueprints and start building.

CHAPTER 21

STUCK IN THE MIDDLE WITH YOU

I'M A CHILD OF THE 70S. Back then, most popular music was played on AM radio. FM was just getting started, and Sirius XM and streaming music was inconceivable. I recall plugging in a twenty-five-foot extension cord from a plug in the garage to get it out to my radio. I'd plug it in and find CKLW out of Detroit, Michigan, to take in AM rock 'n' roll gold. I loved hearing the groups that would one day become legendary acts as well as the fabulous one hit wonders. Every decade has one-hit-wonder acts. I'm sure you have some favorites from the decade where you were in your formative years.

There was a band called Stealers Wheel, which I'm sure is so obscure you'd need to look them up on Google. They were a one-hit wonder from Scotland. One of their vocalists, Gerry Rafferty, did go on to have several solo hits, but the band hit it big once. Their hit was "Stuck in the Middle with You," a song that stays with you long after you hear it, not only for its super catchy melody, but for conjuring an image we all know all too well: surrounded by clowns and jokers and just trying to make sense of it all.

> **Being the manager of others is the most difficult position in any company.**

Being the manager of others is the most difficult position in any company. If you ever ask people managers what they enjoy the most in their role, they'll share all about the responsibilities and scope of their work and authority. They may mention a few people from their team, but they're more comfortable describing the work they produce. The only reason they don't immediately think about their people is the messaging they receive from senior leadership. It's easy to banter about and discuss data, goals, deadlines, and project status reports. We can fill entire days and keep our conversations at this shallow level. Yes, shallow level.

When you can describe your day without mentioning people, it doesn't eliminate their existence. They may be missing from these shallow conversations, but that doesn't make them invisible. Any time you get to meet one-one-one with a manager, the conversation doesn't stay shallow for long. They swim in people all day long. They will tell you that the human aspect of their role is the most challenging because people are unpredictable and they talk back. Isn't it interesting that organizations outwardly express the desire to have employees bring "their entire self to work" . . . but don't be vocal, contrary, or creative. We'd much rather have you come to work, take your place, put your head down, and speak when spoken to. Too harsh? Not really because that is the behavior that is allowed in organizations more that we're freely willing to admit.

The Theory X approach to management is still prevalent. What is Theory X? In a simplified explanation, Theory X managers want people to shut up, do what they're told, and stay in line. There have been countless programs and efforts to have employees be empowered, engaged and contributory. These have met with varied level of success. Most of these programs are well-defined and well-intentioned. The variability of people being people throws a wrench in empowerment because we are more comfortable when the least amount of variation is present.

The permanence of people being unpredictable leads to managers becoming frustrated. They see employees as a nuisance instead of an asset. In their mind, they see "clowns to the left of me and jokers to the right . . ." and they end up being stuck in the middle. The conundrum that occurs is that managers are positioned with people above and below them. They are literally in the middle. Layer on top of this their relationship with HR. Chances are HR is engaged, or chooses to engage, with managers primarily when problems occur. HR is brought in as a watchdog to investigate, assess, and address difficult behavior. Too often HR is not viewed as a resource to assist managers in working with others; we're sent to clean things up. The implication is that we're called upon to enforce rules and catch people who are out of line. Makes you want to go into HR doesn't it?

I know many HR peers who relish this head knocking role. They get a rush knowing that they're jumping into some fire with the ability to get it put out. I personally feel that if this is how you view HR, you should change occupations. Being the enforcer internally within an organization is a thankless job that only brings about divisiveness. There is a place for us to step in and address employee relations issues. It needs to happen in a constructive and objective manner, not as a self-proclaimed deputy.

Here's a different perspective for you to consider. What if you chose to be "stuck in the middle" with your managers as their ally? What if they had an on-going and productive relationship with you? How would employee relations be addressed if people managers knew you were a true resource instead of a "support function" that was only called upon when deemed necessary?

You can exhibit another facet of leadership by willingly jumping straight into the mix of middle management and supervision. This is far different than establishing yet another "Line to Manager" training initiative. Training is needed so that managers and supervisors are equipped on the people side of their jobs. This never stops. It can't be taught is some six- or ten-week course where peers sit and get lectured for hours at a time. What we've never learned is that when training is pounded into people in short bursts, they still return back to their old way of working. Very little is retained and even less lends itself to sustainable change. I'm not being cynical. I'm being realistic. The pressure of productivity and hitting your numbers will always overcome the best training efforts.

There is a way to make people management enjoyable and successful. However, it will cost you two important things: your personal time in your day and the ability to be a mirror.

The most valuable investment you can give anyone is your time. There's nothing even close. It's the one factor of our lives that we always say we lack, but that's not really true. You will become an incredibly effective HR professional by being a willing giver of your time. Time allows people to share, vent, and work through what is facing them. Your intentional attention will also build deeper relationships than any set of meetings or training courses will ever reach.

When I first started in my current HR role, I spent the first three months listening and observing people. My boss, who I've now reported to for almost a decade and a half, tasked me with this. He told me that I would be tempted to see situations and want to come up with quick solutions. He said that having this approach is natural, and most people feel that is how they're most effective. He asked me to trust him and be patient. He reassured me that I'd have plenty of time to come up with potential solutions to what I found. I listened to his advice even though it was against my nature.

I started to visit our restaurants, and each time I entered one, the team members would freeze. They wondered why someone from corporate was visiting. Something had to be wrong, or even worse, someone was going to get fired. This apprehension extended from the GM to the front line. Our interactions were usually very short, and if I didn't have a set agenda of items to cover, the conversations were awkward and filled with more silence than words. This was difficult for me. I am a talker. I enjoy meeting people and am eager to jump right in with others to chat and learn as much as I can about them. I don't need to do this over a number of visits. I'm ready to go the moment I meet someone new. I know that is not the case of how most people like to initiate encounters. I had to fight another natural tendency in this patience tour, and it was grueling for me. I desperately wanted to strike up a conversation and start learning the manager's interests, hobbies, concerns, and so on. I didn't do that. I stuck to the advice from my boss.

After the initial three-month window, my boss and I sat down, and he asked me for my summary of observations about people. Please note that during this same time frame I was learning my role and the department of team members I had inherited. In other companies, I had always practiced as an HR department of one. So I was learning my people along with the team members across our organization. Our summary review went very well, and he confirmed many of the observations I had seen. He asked me to continue observing others from now on. He didn't want it to be a short-term exercise to move on to more pressing and "important" things.

He also shared with me observations that he had held back because he wanted to see if my time out in the field matched his years of experience. He is an introvert by nature, but you'd never know that because he's warm, engaging, and playful. He takes the time to learn one to two tidbits of personal information of all of the people he works with. He confirmed with me that time is the most valuable gift you can give to others. He had become so practiced at touching base with people that he could work a restaurant in minutes.

Over the years, we continue to have conversations about giving our time to our managers. He is a constant person who nudges me to keep this at the front of what I do as the "HR guy." The aspect that I added to this practice is being the mirror I mentioned earlier. When you take time to meet with and chat with managers, you'll notice their interest and energy perk up. They're looking for a lifeline to provide an escape valve for all of the people stuff they're facing.

When I go out into pizzerias now, there is very little apprehension. I have easy conversations with the majority of people working, and I usually get focused time with the manager who is on shift. The conversations range from personal stories and experiences to work items. I enjoy this aspect of my job more than any other. I've noticed the managers enjoy it as well. However, when I leave the restaurant, that managers fall back into their "production first" mode within minutes. They don't feel they have the latitude or support from the company to spend time with team members just like they do with me. Also, it isn't a natural behavior for them to have conversations with their staff. Team members look at them as authority figures, and they are.

When I saw this happening time after time, I told the managers that they need to be mirrors. If they enjoyed spending time with me, then they needed to recognize that their team members wanted that same experience and attention. It didn't need to mimic our relationship, but they had to make themselves accessible and approachable to listen and hear people out. Just like they didn't like it when I first visited them with the expectation that the only reason we would talk is about issues, their staff wouldn't want every conversation to be about issues either.

Being a mirror is tough, and it takes practice. To encourage and enable our managers to learn this behavior, I've made it a practice to regularly visit them during their shifts and at their restaurants. I've taken the stance that the best use of my time is investing in them. Now, I can already hear the objections from you as a reader that I just don't understand that you don't have that freedom in how HR is practiced where you work. I do understand. I have experienced companies trying to limit my time with others. It bites, and it's unfortunate.

To counter that, I encourage you to start small. Reach out to those with whom you work closely. Start investing your time with them and add more and more people over time. This isn't a matter of spending hours and hours of your day doing this. It's a matter of minutes and minutes. Intentional time doesn't mean extensive time. It just means that the use of your time is focused and meant to connect.

Get in the middle of your managers. It's where they live. The more you do this, the clowns and jokers will no longer be there, and your managers will see the great people they work with every day.

CHAPTER 22

BE A TRAILBLAZER

OVER YOUR CAREER, chances are that you're going to work for more than one company and occupy more than one HR role. There are some companies that still have a culture of long-tenured employees, but they are the exception. Career mobility is now the new norm. It's not uncommon to see people have three, five, seven, or more jobs throughout their career. There are many factors that can lead to this, and they vary based on each person's experience, how the company is performing, and how they view and utilize the human resources function. When people have changed jobs in the past, the company they worked for was usually the instigator of such a move. People didn't change jobs much if they didn't have to. The generations that have been entering the workforce recently are creating a shift in job transition because they're willing to leave at any time and they may, or may not, have a set reason.

With careers becoming more fluid in HR, we need to recognize that this is also occurring across all industries. We now work at companies for a season ourselves, and that is true for many employees.

I've been very fortunate to have worked at the same company for the past thirteen years. I don't take it for granted. One quick aside for context. This is my fifth HR role in a different company over my more than thirty-year career. This is the longest I've worked at any company. Ironically, even though I've been at this company for almost a decade and a half, this length of tenure is still considered "new" to many whom I work with. It's true. I get to regularly celebrate anniversaries with our team members, and it's not uncommon to have people reach their 15th, 20th, 25th, 30th and even 40+ year milestone. I joined one of those "exception" companies where long tenure is acceptable and even revered with respect.

An environment with so much tenure has its advantages and disadvantages. The advantages are obvious. You get to work with amazing, talented individuals who offer stability and consistency both personally and organizationally. It's also very comforting to head to work and see folks you enjoy being with. You get to go through life with many of them by sharing in life events with your fellow employees, including families growing, kids graduating, weddings, and even funerals. When you have this much tenure you do actually become that "family" company so many people wish to have.

The disadvantage to a company having such extensive tenure is that you can easily get into a rut of thinking. It's easy to take things at face value because you're around the same people every day. You may question things less because everyone seems to be "on the same page." (My least favorite corporate phrase.) You don't even realize that you're following in step because it's your daily norm.

My boss and I have a weekly check-in, which we've done since I've been at the company. It's a great time to catch up on projects, HR items, team member issues, and life. We didn't know that we were being so forward-thinking, since check-ins and regular feed-back are the newest craze in HR circles. I guess we didn't realize it because it was the best way for us to stay connected and do our jobs well.

The key to these meetings is that we've always been open and candid with each other. That's refreshing and challenging at the same time. I don't think we could have made it successfully over the years I've been with the company if that wasn't a founda-tional expectation of our meetings. A little over a year ago, we had one of those challenging conversations.

My company has been very supportive of my involvement in the greater HR community. That's been true when I've been in roles locally, at the state level, and nationally. I'm so grateful that I've been able to see what other companies do and how they practice HR and business overall. I've seen small companies, large com-panies, massive metropolises, and rural villages in my travels. Meeting with other business professionals from this broad mix of backgrounds has allowed me to witness and learn in ways I never could have by staying put inside our four walls alone.

My boss said, "You know you go to these events all over and hear and see all kinds of approaches to work." I agreed. Then he said,

"Funny, you seem to be becoming more like us. I don't hear those different ideas and viewpoints much anymore."

That was it. That was all that needed to be said. I sat there silently because he was right. I had fallen into the pattern that tenure can lead to and didn't even notice.

Before I joined my current company, I worked for another great boss. When I told her that I was going to change jobs and leave her after nine years, we just wept. I had gone into her office to tell her that I found this new career opportunity and didn't even manage to get one word out. The moment I saw her, I burst into tears. She knew what I was trying to express. We hugged, and I don't even remember giving my two-week notice to her then. She asked where I was going to go and what I was going to be doing. I was so close to her that words wouldn't adequately express how much she had meant to me and my career.

A few weeks after I had left to take on my new HR role, I received a card from her in the mail with a quote in it from the poet Ralph Waldo Emerson. It said:

"Do not go where the path may lead, go instead where there is no path and leave a trail."

When I read it, I wept again and taped it to my office wall. She added a note inside the card which read: "I saw this and thought of you. Always remember to make new trails."

It was great advice then, and it still is today. You see, we can blaze new trails in our organizations from both an HR and a business perspective. It's easy for us to lose sight of this, and too often we feel we don't have the time or energy to go where there is no path. That shouldn't be the case. We shouldn't be lulled into any pattern at work that dulls us or keeps us just plodding along.

HR was meant to drive change. I know that even typing this, many will disagree. I will hold to this belief though. We can look at the various human interactions which occur in every department and make suggestions on possible solutions. We have the ability to gracefully guide others so that people are in alignment in order to perform at their best. This often means changing the path and making a new one so others can follow the trail.

When I look back over my career, I recall times when I created and established significant milestones that altered the direction of how HR was viewed and practiced. Those big successes are few and far between. It's easy for us to defend and point back to the past efforts we accomplished. We may feel that we're in a place where a new path isn't possible. At that time, we need to evaluate if it's time to make one of those career changes outside our current company.

Whenever there are no new paths to explore, then understand that you're going to remain in a never-ending loop that will keep circling and circling with no tangible start or end. That isn't healthy for you or your organization. HR should blaze trails. You should look throughout every crevice possible to see what could be refreshed, reevaluated, and modernized. As much as society moves at the speed of light now, so should we. HR can't keep being an anchor that holds people, and companies, back. We should be at the forefront leading with what we bring to the entire organization collectively and through individuals.

One facet that is directly in front of you, and all of the people working at your firm, is this: We need to manage our careers and be a trailblazer to assist other's careers. Since HR is responsible for people throughout their entire life cycle within your company, you can become someone who starts clearing the brush and vines that block the career paths of others. When companies have an HR function that asserts itself in saying that they are the steward of the people, then you are bringing a skill to an organization that is missing.

Guiding people throughout their season with you intentionally will be far more rewarding for them, and their time with the company will be full and robust. If people just float aimlessly from task to task and role to role, we are missing out on enabling them to be the talented people they are meant to be. You can step up to the interworking mechanism of the company and link up with each employee on purpose. Trust me, doing this action will blaze trails in ways you could never have imagined.

Doing this type of work will allow you to have a better perspective on what a person can and cannot do because you're connected to them. It will give you a hands-on viewpoint that is more contextual than only offering programs for people to sign up for. You may see that the best step for someone is to leave the company. Wouldn't it be great if we had such a relationship with our team members that we could even anticipate how, and when, they should move? A fellow HR executive who is a dear friend of mine told me her company practiced that employees should have "a red carpet in and a red carpet out" for how they joined, developed, and transitioned from the company.

I'm sure there are many trails to blaze in your organization and throughout your career. Here's my advice. Start with managing your career and then be cognizant of managing the careers of others. Don't get set in your ways. Evaluate if you're being a trailblazer or if you're following the path that has been set before you. If you're on a path that hasn't changed much, step off and explore new directions. You don't know what great things lay before you!!

CHAPTER 23

PEOPLE MATTER

WHENEVER YOU GATHER a group of people together and ask them what their company views as the most important asset is in the company, the answer is a resounding: *our people*!! This may be described in other ways such as "human capital," "our talented associates," "the people who make up the X Company family," etc. This is a wonderful aspiration, and I'm sure that you can go through the hallways and lobbies of most organizations and see some formal plaque proudly displaying this sentiment. This may even be heard and seen in company meetings and in the on-boarding process for new hires. However, it's not true.

The company's greatest asset is . . . its revenue.

This is the truth. Companies exist because they're able to be profitable. The more profitable they are, the better for on-going existence, investment, and return for their owners and shareholders. This isn't "wrong." We wouldn't have jobs if we worked for companies that weren't financially solvent and hopefully growing. Others wouldn't be able to have jobs either if companies weren't bringing in a constant revenue stream.

If a company were honest enough to put this reality up on their vision and mission statements dotting the various offices, hallways, and lobbies, they would be barbequed by anyone who read it. I can't imagine the negative press that would happen to a company being this bold. Social media would do its best to destroy them. We're about our people, not money!! I'm not sharing this because I'm cynical. This is being realistic. We all work with the hope being that our company has enough profits to stay in business, pay our salaries, and hopefully offer some set of benefits to provide protection for the needs of ourselves and our families. I'm all for that, and I hope you are too.

So, since generating revenue is necessary, can people still be valued at this lofty level? The answer is "Yes," but it may not be in the manner in which it has been traditionally seen and expressed. Companies are made up of humans. Unfortunately, we have been taught to think and act in a compartmentalized fashion. Every function within a company desperately seeks to position itself as vital, indispensable, and independent. They may recognize the need to work with other departments, but only as needed. It's more important to show your strength and vitality than it is your collaboration and interdependence. We may think that people are valued if they work directly with us. We can vouch for those people because we interact with them and see their work. We have little desire or reason to engage people across an organization. It may occur on a project, but we can't wait to circle back into the group with whom we identify most.

A multitude of compartments acting like little kingdoms is challenging because each one is needed to make the company be as successful as possible. There have to be people who see across the enterprise who can move levers up, down, in, and out in order to keep the company moving as a complete organism. We can't afford for any one compartment to be so dominant that it keeps the ecosystem of the company unbalanced. That may be needed at times, but in the end, the various groups need to settle back into a fairly stable environment.

Those in senior leadership should scan the horizon to see how the whole is or isn't preforming and assist in that lever moving in order to keep the continuum of work fluid. However, senior leaders can fall into a pattern of lording over their area of business and not seeing the need to work effectively with other departments. I have seen this happen in every company I've worked for. When a certain senior leader is the strongest voice or performer, they can keep the entire company focused on them. They don't seek balance. They seek, and enjoy, power. This may be useful for certain time periods when a company is in crisis, but it can't be sustained. People will get fed up with this imbalance and clamor for change, or they'll see that this power struggle isn't going to budge, and they'll leave the company.

HR also has to keep its eyes focused on the horizon. I know that this may also sound aspirational and seem out of reach, but it needs to become the reality for human resources. The reason for this is that we can change the messaging from people being our "greatest asset" to a more operational approach by showing that "people matter."

When you look up the definition of the word "matter," the verb definition captures the essence of what this term can mean for an organization. Things that matter "have significance and are of importance" according to the *Oxford English Dictionary*. Yet again. HR has the responsibility to make sure that the people who work in their company "have significance and are of importance." This has to become non-negotiable for our roles and our profession. To make the "people matter" culture come to life, our approach to who we are and what we do needs to shift.

I understand that in laying out this ideal in the following paragraphs, I may be speaking out of turn. This goal may seem foreign and out of reach in your current HR role. There are far too many companies who keep HR in a small, confined box. It may be hard to break out of the current circumstance that you're experiencing. Your company may also dismiss these suggestions if you chose to practice them yourself or if you try to discuss them internally. I wish this wasn't the case.

Here's something to keep in mind. I feel if companies don't become organizations that are genuinely people-centric and show that people matter, then they will cease to be relevant. They may exist today, but they won't be around in the future. I'm not trying to predict the downfall of the workplace with some doom and gloom prophecy. I just know that companies that are people-centric are more agile, adept, and able to bend, flex, and completely reinvent themselves much easier than those who chose not to be.

One other item to note. This isn't an either/or position where you throw yourself on a sword if a company doesn't respond or embrace a "people matter" approach holistically. You can have incredible impact and influence when you're able get this established at an individual level and even in small pockets. Once a "people matter" approach takes hold with someone, it can't help but grow. It won't be contained. You may hit some significant resistance in taking this to be the culture of the whole organization, but it's worth the fight.

A people matter culture begins with HR. This is true because we are the one group within a company who gets to work with all of the wonderful humans across the organization. People have to *matter* to you in order for you to be the best HR practitioner possible. This can't be a sentiment, program, or cute motivational poster. When people matter, it will show in your behavior and approach.

There are some key areas where you can put yourself in the best position of establishing and sustaining a "people matter" culture. First, you need to be a vulnerable, authentic, genuine, and flawed person yourself. You can't put on the "HR face" when going out to interact with people, or when they come to meet with you. We must be humans ourselves. Don't mistake this as the hollow "put the 'H' back in HR." Being human should never have left our practice. Whoever thought that was a good idea has led us down a path which has only led us to being isolated and

> **A people matter culture begins with HR.**

ignored. When people see that you're as normal as they are, then you will start sowing the seeds of credibility. We're all a bit flawed, awkward, and quirky. That's what makes people so amazing. We were never meant to be robots who lack feelings because of some inordinate fear that people will take advantage of us or the company. When you start being human yourself, you'll see that people have always mattered to you. You'll be more comfortable in your skin and will once again start enjoying being an HR professional.

Second, you need to know that you'll be asked to push against the establishment. You may read this recommendation and want to back out. I know this is hard, but leadership is not meant to be without risks. HR has the responsibility of being the voice of every person from the CEO to the person working on the front line. There are no sides. There are only people. In looking out for every person, you can better look at every angle of situations. You may land on the company side in one circumstance, and against it in another. Pushing against the establishment means that you will challenge the norms when needed. You have the ability to help people, and the whole company, evolve. People can't "matter" if you only represent a certain small faction of them. We're here for everyone: the performer and the one who is struggling. Every. Single. Person.

Third, be intentional. There's no reason for us to keep thinking that we'll make an impact or be leaders if we keep trying to lure people to the conclusion we're trying to reach by hints, innuendos, and coaxing. It doesn't make you less empathetic by being decisive. You aren't going to become this harsh taskmaster. Your inner being will remain intact. This is where HR should take a page from how others act in organizations. I'm sure you'll have no shortage of examples of people you work with who are far too direct. Intentionality allows you to step in on behalf of others. You'll need to do this in a "people matter" culture. We should do our best to make sure that people aren't overlooked, trampled, or forgotten. Senior leadership desires HR folks who are willing to stand their ground. Being intentional takes practice, and you may surprise others when you start doing this consistently. They may think that HR isn't capable. It's time to break that expectation and set a new one.

Finally, be present. When people matter, they deserve your full attention. You have the time to make this happen. It isn't the time suck that you feel it will be. Being present gives you the full picture of what people are facing. It will enable you to gather information, assess all of the angles, and help make the best decision available. Eliminating distractions when you're in the middle of engaging others may be challenging since we're pulled in so many different directions. Remember this – they are too. We're not unique because we work in HR. Everyone is being yanked in too many directions. Breathe and clear your head to give someone a few moments of undivided attention. When you do this, you'll gain another attribute of an effective leader. Presence isn't needed only for employee relations items. Presence is needed because it shows people that they matter.

How you design a "people matter" culture is in the hands of HR. You know the culture you currently have, and you can imagine what it would look like by becoming people-centric. There is no quick fix or formula that can be applied to your role. The desire to see this come to life is the best place to start. Exhibiting the attributes of being human yourself, pushing against the norms, being intentional, and being present are arrows in your quiver that can be gently launched when needed. People matter. It's time to make that a reality and not an aspiration.

CHAPTER 24

DEVELOP
YOURSELF FIRST

I WONDER IF Theodor Geisel thought he'd change the world by creating worlds of imagination drawn together with rhymes. You know his by his pen name Dr. Seuss. His children's books have been read out loud to generations of children. I remember my mom, who was a teacher for her entire career, would sit down with me and read classics like *The Cat in the Hat* and *One Fish, Two Fish, Red Fish, Blue Fish*. She read many others to my brother and me when we were little. When she took the time to read to us every night, it showed us how enjoyable reading was. It is one of my fondest memories.

The Dr. Seuss books soon became favorites to read on my own. I tried to memorize several of them and was fascinating by characters like the Lorax, Thidwick the Big-Hearted Moose, Sam-I-Am, the Cat in the Hat, the Grinch, Horton, and the miniature people known as Whos. As I got older, I kept my love of reading going. Sure, I read books because they were assigned, but I would have two to three other books going at the same time just for fun. I took a class in college on Oral Interpretation where Dr. Seuss came back into my life. In this class, we took existing written works and we'd have to research them and be prepared to stand in front of the class and recite passages using our interpretations. One of my classmates chose to recite an extended passage from the classic *Green Eggs and Ham*, and everyone chimed in once the pattern of where the eggs could be eaten were shared. He got an A+ for his interpretation because it was brilliant!!

Dr. Seuss once said, "The more that you read, the more things you will know. The more that you learn, the more places you'll go."

This quote seems a bit simplistic and stating the obvious, but I'm sure Dr. Seuss wrote it because he saw that people around him don't read as much as they used to. When we were children, our imaginations were unlimited and unfettered. We'd make up things that had no possibility of becoming reality. That never stopped us. We'd keep coming up with ideas just because they popped into our heads. Our parents would listen to our colorful creations with patience. I know that sometime adults would try to squelch these far-fetched scenarios, but we had quite a bit of freedom to let our imaginations soar for the first five or six years of our lives.

Then, we went to school. Attending school was essential because you'd started to be exposed to more and more information that you'd never be able to gather on your own. You also began to learn the existence of social constructs and how people viewed each other. The school playground provided a robust laboratory of the good and bad side of human behavior. You were introduced to judgement, stereotypes, generalizations, and social cliques. The more structure that came into your life, the more your imagination dimmed. Chances are you fell in line with the rest of your classmates, and it became more and more difficult to be creative and come up with ideas that fell outside the boundaries of how everyone acted and thought.

What's funny is that schooling was meant to prepare us for "life." I remember hearing that expression being shared from many teachers and school administrators. That was their justification for layers and layers of rules and the use of bells that moved from one location to another in an orderly fashion. I think the educators should have told us that they were preparing us for work and not life.

We had so many subjects to learn, homework to complete, and extracurricular activities that having free time to develop myself just got squeezed out. The further I went in my education; the more and more constricted learning became. I learned a ton of information over the years, but more often than not, it was to get prepared for an exam. Once the exam was completed, I moved on to the next set of information. I'm sure I retained some things, but the goal was to learn enough to obtain a good grade. Passing exams led to earning a degree which allowed me to get a job in the field I was pursuing. Please note that college was the path I chose to take. I understand, and admire, people that end up in their career through a multitude of paths. What's intriguing is that we all learned in our own fashion and pathway solely to land a job. Once we obtained a job, we were done.

Don't think that's true? Then, why do we need to have development programs in our organizations? Why do we need to learn on top of work? Shouldn't it be a natural occurrence versus a concerted effort?

It should be, but that's not how companies view things. The expectation of companies is that people show up and work. There is far more focus and attention on visibility, attendance, and productivity than there is on growth and development. If that wasn't the case, you wouldn't have to create development and training programs. The company would see the value in having people grow, and they would build development into their company's fabric.

Development also faces another internal obstacle because many view it as taking away from daily productivity and costing too much. There is very little legwork done to prove, or disprove, this feeling. It's usually the opinion which is shared out loud, so development gets stifled. Companies may invest in on-the-job training and skill development, which does have tangible value, but they hesitate to cater to personal development. If efforts can be bundled into mass and scale, then it will get attention and funding. This is archaic. The workforce of today wants every aspect of their job to be personalized. That will sound unreasonable to the traditional hierarchies which still run most organizations. What we're missing is that personalization is going on all around us. It's how people take in information, entertainment and conduct commerce. Large group lecture-based classroom training exists, but it's not how people are consuming information.

We are so entrenched with how we were taught and learned that we don't know how to break from the model we experienced. Instead of trying to meet people where they are and how they're doing life, we stick to the tried and true approaches. I know that technology has replaced much of the in-person classroom training, but it is still happening on a mass scale more than in an environment where a person can design their own development path. What is there to fear? Isn't it more beneficial for our employees to learn than it is for us to control how they learn?

I think there's another obstacle that inhibits development of others, and that is that we look at training and development as necessary for others only. We don't take care of ourselves HR. We're so busy making sure that some form of training and development is happening throughout every other area in our companies that we stop learning. I understand that each of us has a full plate. It's probably overflowing, and you're behind more than you are ahead. How in the world can you make time for yourself? It just seems so out of reach. I want you to consider a different perspective regarding this.

You can't develop others unless you develop yourself.

When I began my career, I never even considered further development. I had been in school for seventeen years before I took on my first HR role. I wanted to be done as much as my employer wanted me to sit at my desk and work. I have to admit that this was how I viewed HR for over the first half of my career. I'm ashamed to say that because those are years when I could have been learning and growing. I was definitely gaining an education based on experience, and I'm thankful for that. Looking back now, I could

> **You can't develop others unless you develop yourself.**

have been even more impactful if I had been intentional in my own personal development.

My career started taking a different path when a colorful memo came across my desk about a local HR Roundtable. I felt the urge to get outside the confines of my company and attend. Taking that small first step opened my eyes once again as if I was that child sitting in my mom's lap eagerly waiting for her to read another Dr. Seuss book. When I realized there was an entire HR community that had been in existence forever, I never looked back. I started to become involved in my local HR SHRM chapter and attended meetings to learn. I then asked if I could start going to larger events and conferences. As a department of one, I explained that I needed to attend these gatherings because I didn't have a way to keep current inside the company. This was true, but my intention was also to keep fanning the flame of development. I started meeting peers who were in HR and that led to even more development opportunities.

In the late 2000s, the advent of social media arrived. Now, I could read blogs written by people both in my field or in non-related fields. I started to become visible and active on social media platforms myself, and the world of knowledge accessible to me broadened once again. Recently, the dawn of podcasts has begun. It seems that the methods of learning and the expansion of available knowledge keeps evolving. That isn't daunting; it's exciting!!

The key to learning from social media is understanding your capacity. You don't have to get as involved as those you see who are active. This isn't a matter of replicating the activity of others. It's more important that you view social media as another way to communicate. Don't view social media as a competition because when you spend more time comparing, you'll find yourself withdrawing from a vast sea of content and information. Find the platforms where you feel most at ease and participate to the level you feel comfortable. There is so much great content merely one click away that can make you an even more talented business professional. The key is to make sure you are connected to these resources yourself.

I am very active in social media personally because I understand my capacity. I look to connect and learn across several platforms. I regularly read and subscribe to over 140 blogs, tweet on a daily basis, write a blog, and participate in Twitter chats. I attend conferences to speak to my peers and also go to classes to continue to learn as much as I can. I share my level of participation because personal professional development is a priority for me. Being this active has established a base from which to show others in my company the power and value of developing others. I don't have programs anymore. I'm trying to create a personalized experience for people to learn, grow, fail, and develop based on who they are and how they best learn.

I'm not going to list a certain step method for you to mimic. I want to encourage you to reawaken that child who loved to read and learn in yourself. When you find what works best for you, step in and seek personal and professional development. The more you learn, the more current and relevant you will remain in your role and in your organization. You'll soon see that Dr. Seuss was right. You'll start finding new places to learn, grow, and go.

CHAPTER 25

TAG, YOU'RE IT !!

WHEN KIDS ARE JUST TODDLERS they are amazed by the gift of mobility. It doesn't take much time for a child go from wobbling across the room to a full-on sprint. Once they realize that walking can be accentuated with speed, they run everywhere. I'm sure if we could look inside their minds, we'd see that they think they are traveling at some insane speed even though they are very easy to catch and scoop up in your arms. The key to their constant running is a sense of complete freedom. They are unencumbered by any concern or worry. Their only thought is to be in the moment and run. You need to keep an eye out for these little sprinters, and the other thing you'll notice is that they squeal and laugh in an unabandoned fashion. They don't know, or care, that anyone is watching.

It's funny to see parents react when they see their child running as if they are sure to escape. Fear covers their face, and they are embarrassed by the behavior of their child. They grab them as quickly as humanly possible and scold them for being so reckless. Isn't that sad? Instead of embracing the unadulterated joy and encouraging the running child, we seek to repress their joy. Thankfully, small children have short memories. The impulse and excitement to run the instant their parent puts them down pulls them straight back into the exhilaration they had just moments before. The feeling they experienced far outweighs any rule of proper behavior they are breaking.

When's the last time you had that sense of joy and freedom? I'm sure you could share times when you went on vacation and had some awe-inspiring moments that gave you a glimpse of what you used to do often when you were younger. Each time we have one of those mountaintop experiences, we long to hold onto the feeling for as long as possible. We don't want it to fade and disappear, but it does.

What if you decided that you no longer wanted to be mired in a world, or occupation, filled with stress, frustration, and futility? Do you think it's possible? I do.

If you're in a place where being in HR is more of a burden than something you look forward to, you need to make a decision. Is it time to find some other profession to practice? Or are you going to step into being a leader in your role and throughout your organization? You could also decide that you want to stay in HR, but you may need to change where you work and who you work for.

Regardless of which question applies to you, you need to decide. When HR chooses to settle and exist in a state that is hovers around mediocrity, you're not helping yourself or your company. The role of any employee in a company should be to perform so that they're adding value with the goal of seeing the company thrive and move forward. Maintaining the status quo isn't a good option. Being the parent who scoops up and corrects the child is far more disappointing than being the child who runs with an endless horizon laid out before them.

I've been in the position where I practiced HR as the person responsible for constricting, correcting, and berating people to conform and get in their place. I was as miserable as they were. I didn't know that I could stand up, push back, and reset what my role, and HR, could become. When I remembered the joy that had eluded me after I "grew up," I did what I could to change this reality to frame a potential new outcome. Taking steps to no longer be a function viewed as a "necessary evil" took courage and the willingness to take some lumps along the way. There were many times that I stumbled, failed, and became discouraged. But once I learned to run again like that toddler, I never stopped. Whenever I had someone try to discourage me and put me back in my place, I just waited until they set me down and I took off again.

Please note that I'm not encouraging you to be destructive or negligent, or to act in a manner that ever puts others at a disadvantage just so you can succeed. In fact, I mean just the opposite. I approach each day with a positive outlook and watch the horizon stretch out in front of me eager to see what the day will bring. The areas I've described throughout this book aren't just colorful tales. I use these attributes, efforts, and characteristics to be someone who leads from where I am. The different concepts can be utilized regardless of your level within your organization. Remember: if people are around, you can practice HR!!

Throughout my childhood I grew up in small, rural towns. Those included the mighty metropolises of Luckey, Gibsonburg and Ada, Ohio. They're categorized as villages, which means that each of them has under 5,000 people as inhabitants. When I grew up, I spent far more time outside any house than I did inside one. I understand that it was a different time with far less technology. Having "less" didn't inhibit me, or my friends, from being kids filled with boundless imagination and energy. Since we were outside, we relied on playing games that involved running, hiding, and a sense of adventure.

Most of the time these games involved a group of other kids that sometimes included siblings or cousins. We'd use the phone fixed to a wall to call and determine a place and time to gather. That was about the extent of our planning. Once everyone found their way to a common meeting place, there would be loud arguing trying to decide what game we'd all play. The extroverts (we didn't know that term then) would be the loudest and would make enough noise to get some sort of consensus, and a game would be chosen. Some of these games involved picking teams. Those were great, but you ran the risk of excluding some people or hurting their feelings if they were chosen last. Whenever I was able to be the loudest voice, I'd make the suggestion to play Tag.

Tag is one of the best games ever created. One person is "it" and you chase everyone else trying to tag them to pass on being "it." Inevitably we'd add on unnecessary rules because someone felt that people weren't playing fair, or someone has some advantage over others. They were harmless and never grounded in logic. Once everyone agreed to some new rule, the game would take off once again. We would run, scream, laugh, dodge, and carry on for hours until we dropped from exhaustion.

At the end of one of these sessions, we'd all say our goodbyes and plan to get together again the next day to play once again.

I miss those days. When I played with all of my peers back then, we were almost recreating the same abandon you see in those running toddlers. We couldn't wait to gather. Almost every day was filled with camaraderie and a sense of togetherness because we had each other, and we played.

HR, I'm calling out to you to come join me. I want you to enjoy what you do as an HR professional and run with unfettered abandon. You can be a leader. I know it because I've seen it myself and in others. It doesn't matter what type of industry you're in or whether you're just starting out in your career. You could be an HR coordinator or a CHRO. You have the ability to take the human resources efforts of your company to heights it has never seen. We can build and create people-centric organizations where HR is an integrated and essential resource that initiates tangible activity leading to sustainable results. By keeping a culture alive where we consider people first and recognize that people matter, we will create a company that attracts, retains, and develops talent. Those types of companies will flourish. HR was meant to lead. You were meant to lead.

Take heart before you join in. Remember that any great game of tag needs to have

> **HR was meant to lead. *You* were meant to lead.**

multiple players. You aren't alone. There are literally thousands of HR peers around the planet who are longing to know and connect with you. This game of tag is being played on a global playground. It doesn't matter if you're an HR department of one or if you work in an HR function made up of several people over several locations. If you are practicing HR in some form, you're a part of the game and a phenomenally supportive community.

It's time to play the game. Everyone's running. Look out. Tag, you're it!!

CONCLUSION

ONE LAST STORY . . .

I was fortunate a few years ago to go with my son and five other
Boy Scouts and an additional dad to a national camp in the
Florida Keys called Sea Base. It was an incredible week filled with
a series of adventures. Whenever you attend one of these camps,
you're reminded that the boys are in charge and you're just along
for the ride. They decide what activities they want to do and the
schedule of when everything will happen, and the adults aren't
consulted at all.

One of the options they chose was to go deep sea fishing. We
gathered early Wednesday morning of our week-long jaunt and
piled into this massive motorboat. The weather was perfect
with azure blue skies set alight from the blazing sun. Everyone
was anxious to see what this experience was going to be like
because our boat captain was a bit of a loose cannon. Captain
Steve (not this author) was a gregarious and grizzled sea creature.
He couldn't wait to get us out on the water to all become sea-
soned fishermen.

The moment we cleared the "no wake" zone, he opened the
throttle and the massive engines jumped to life. He howled with
laughter as we all tumbled over each other as the front of the
boat lifted into the air and we skimmed across the water's surface like a skipping stone. We settled down a bit so the boat could
cut through the ocean's waves. Captain Steve explained that we
would all be catching fish this day and he expected each scout
and the two adults to be engaged, alert, and involved. He was so
welcoming and convincing that everyone nodded in agreement
to be successful this day. We traveled for a little over 30 minutes
away from any visible land until we were completely surrounded
by churning water only.

Captain Steve then gave us all a surprise as our trip took what we
thought was an ominous turn. He cut the power to the engines
and let the boat bob up and down in the waves. Then he yelled
"Captain overboard!!" and threw himself over the edge of the boat,
disappearing under the water. We all gasped and leaned over the
side of the boat, desperately looking for any sign of him. After a

few minutes, his head popped up and he was a good 200 feet from the boat.

"Over here boys. Jump on in. You need to see this!!" he exclaimed.

We all exchanged nervous glances, and no one moved. He continued to invite us to jump into the ocean, where you couldn't see anything but a deep, blue surface for miles around you. We were in the middle of nowhere, and he was our only hope to get us somewhere safe. He wouldn't come back to the boat until someone joined him. He assured us that we were fine and to trust him. He tried to encourage us by telling us that we'd never have this type of experience again.

I could see that we were at an impasse and someone had to act. So I stood on the side of the rocking boat and hurled myself toward the blue abyss. I could hear the boys scream their disagreement with my decision before I hit the water. I completely sank under the waves and was immersed in warmth and a smooth current. I popped up near Captain Steve, who had a smile that covered his entire face.

"Look down," he said. "You won't believe what you see."

I looked down and saw my feet and churning legs easily moving back and forth as clearly as if I were standing on dry land. The view was incredible. I couldn't believe how transparent the water was.

"Pretty amazing isn't it? You're treading water in the Gulf Stream right now. We're several miles from land, but you can't see something like this unless you're right in the middle of it. This never gets old." Captain Steve wanted me to feel the same sense of awe and the joy he experienced.

I yelled back to the boat and told the boys they should listen to Captain Steve and swim out in the Gulf Stream. I agreed that we would likely never get this chance again. All the boys jumped in, but the other dad stayed on board, which was probably a good idea. We all splashed and swam for several minutes, then headed back on board. The sun continued to shine down on us and we dried quickly. The rest of our fishing adventure was successful; each of us caught at least one fish and several caught many fish. We needed them as our meal for that night when we arrived at an island to camp.

We in HR now find ourselves similarly venturing into uncharted waters by choosing to be leaders in our organizations as well as great practitioners. We're at a place where there's only water and no visible shoreline. The question before you is this—"Will you take the leap over the edge and leave the boat?"

Taking this jump requires a mix of faith and a willingness to take on risk. Leadership is made up of these two components in equal amounts. Much of what we do in our work is unpredictable and unknown. We need to be comfortable with this reality and quit putting in so much effort to attempt what we perceive as control. It's time we took on the mantle of leadership ourselves and put in the effort to have others jump off the boat and join us in the flow of work that ebbs, flows, and swirls all around us daily. We cannot remain stuck in our corners of presumed safety and comfort and still think we can be effective.

So go ahead and jump overboard. I'm here in the water looking to join you in the adventures that lie ahead. Together, as leaders who make a difference, when the water rises, we all rise.

Together we are HR Rising!!

INDEX

ABOUT THE AUTHOR

AN ACCOMPLISHED SPEAKER, WRITER, AND THOUGHT LEADER ON HUMAN RESOURCE MANAGEMENT FOR MORE THAN 30 YEARS, STEVE BROWNE IS DEDICATED TO CONNECTING THE GLOBAL HR COMMUNITY AND HELPING IT LEARN AND GROW TOGETHER.

Browne has held HR roles in various industries, including manufacturing, consumer products, professional services, and restaurants. He is a member of the Society for Human Resource Management (SHRM) Board of Directors and has been a Membership Advisory Council representative for the North Central Region of SHRM and a past Ohio State Council Director. He facilitates a monthly HR roundtable, the weekly HR Internet forum "HR Net," and a nationally recognized HR blog, Everyday People (www.sbrowne.hr.com).

ADDITIONAL SHRM-PUBLISHED BOOKS

Preventing Workplace Harassment in a #MeToo World: A Guide to Cultivating a Harassment-Free Culture
Bobbi K. Dominick, Esq.

California Employment Law: An Employer's Guide, Revised & Updated for 2020
James J. McDonald, Jr.

The SHRM Essential Guide to Employment Law: A Handbook for HR Professionals, Managers, Businesses, and Organizations
Charles H. Fleischer

Developing Business Acumen SHRM Competency Series: Making an Impact in Small Business HR
Jennifer Currence

Applying Critical Evaluation SHRM Competency Series: Making an Impact in Small Business HR
Jennifer Currence

Mastering Consultation as an HR Practitioner
Jennifer Currence

From Hello to Goodbye: Proactive Tips for Maintaining Positive Employee Relations, Second Edition
Christine V. Walters

The Practical Guide to HR Analytics: Using Data to Inform, Transform & Empower HR Decisions
Shonna D. Waters, Valerie N. Streets, Lindsay A. McFarlane, and Rachael Johnson-Murray

HR on Purpose: Developing Deliberate People Passion
Steve Browne

The Price of Pettiness: Bad Behavior in the Workplace and How to Stomp it Out
Alex Alonso

A Manager's Guide to Developing Competencies in HR Staff
Phyllis G. Hartman

Extinguish Burnout: A Practical Guide to Prevention and Recovery
Rob & Terri Bogue

The HR Career Guide: Great Answers to Tough Career Questions
Martin Yate

Ace Your SHRM Certification Exam: A Guide to Success on the SHRM-CP® and SHRM-SCP® Exams
Nancy A. Woolever, editor

The Talent Fix: A Leader's Guide to Recruiting Great Talent
Tim Sackett

Motivation-Based Interviewing: A Revolutionary Approach to Hiring the Best
Carol Quinn

The Recruiter's Handbook: A Complete Guide for Sourcing, Selecting, and Engaging the Best Talent
Sharlyn Lauby

The Power of Stay Interviews for Engagement and Retention, Second Edition
Richard P. Finnegan

Predicting Business Success: Using Smarter Analytics to Drive Results
Scott Mondore, Hannah Spell, Matt Betts, and Shane Douthitt

From WE WILL to AT WILL: A Handbook for Veteran Hiring, Transitioning, and Thriving in the Workplace
Justin Constantine

Investing in People: Financial Impact of Human Resource Initiatives, Third Edition
Wayne F. Cascio, John W. Boudreau, and Alexis A. Fink

Solve Employee Problems Before They Start: Resolving Conflict in the Real World
Scott Warrick

Actualized Leadership: Meeting Your Shadow & Maximizing Your Potential
William L. Sparks

The 9 Faces of HR: A Disruptor's Guide to Mastering Innovation and Driving Real Change
Kris Dunn

Digital HR: A Guide to Technology-Enabled Human Resources
Deborah D. Waddill